# FINDING INTIMACY

# FINDING INTIMACY

## The Art of Happiness in Living Together

## Herbert G. Zerof

WINSTON PRESS

To Aletta and our children — Linda and Cheryl

This edition is published by arrangement with
Random House, Inc.

Library of Congress Catalog Card Number: 81-51162
ISBN: 0-86683-618-7 (previously ISBN: 0-394-42824-2)
Printed in the United States of America
5    4    3    2

Winston Press, Inc.
430 Oak Grove
Minneapolis, Minnesota 55403

# Acknowledgments

EVERY TIME A DISTRESSED COUPLE SHARE THEIR DEEPEST thoughts and feelings with me I feel that I am on hallowed ground. I have learned that compassion comes easy as I try to help them in their private turmoil, and it is from this experience that I have learned the most.

The internal struggles of many of the couples I have known are portrayed in this book, but the external trappings have been altered to protect their identities. It is to these people in their search for intimacy that I owe a special debt of gratitude.

Apart from other distinctions, Philadelphia is the birthplace of one of the first marriage counseling clinics in the United States. It was there that I first learned this unusual art. Emily Mudd, Ph.D., the eminent pioneer of marriage counseling and founder of the Marriage Council of Philadelphia, was one of my mentors. Kenneth Appel, M.D., former president of the American Psychiatric Association, who was strongly supportive of this fledgling discipline as chairman of the Department of Psychiatry, University of Pennsylvania School of Medicine, also added a great deal to my knowledge.

Special thanks are also due Hilda Goodwin, D.S.W., former director of training of the Marriage Council and professor in the Department of Psychiatry, University of Pennsylvania School of Medicine, for providing a creative spark to my career. Charles Schober, M.D., my analyst, first helped me to explore fully the inner world of experience and to know what it means to struggle with dilemmas from the patient's side.

Lastly, Aletta, my wife of nineteen years who is still my good friend, typed the manuscript in its entirety.

# Contents

# Introduction

PEOPLE HAVE ALWAYS HAD PROBLEMS IN LIVING TOGETHER, and always will. However, fifteen or twenty years ago when cohabitation was still primarily called marriage, the difficulties seemed relatively uncomplicated. Spouses had orderly problems which could be solved by traditional means, and which could be neatly compartmentalized. Nostalgia buffs will remember the days when people talked this way:

"What can I do with my mother-in-law?"

"How do you work out a budget?"

"How can I get my wife to undress in the same room with me?"

"How many years of marriage should you wait before having your first child?"

"I want my husband to open the door for me, and be more polite. What can I do?"

Although vestiges of all these problems remain, today, they are expressed differently, less naïvely and more overwhelmingly. The most common complaints brought to a marriage counselor's office today sound this way:

"I don't love him anymore and I'm going to leave him."

"She's still having an affair and I can't stop her."

"We argue all the time. How can we communicate?"

"How can I get him to have oral sex with me?"

"We're bored together. I thought switching partners with our neighbors would be fun, but she won't agree."

"I want a divorce, but he says he'll take me to court and get the children."

"We've been living together three years, and I want a family, but she won't marry me."

Rapid cultural changes today, graphically documented by Alvin Toffler in *Future Shock*, force companions to deal with one another on more sophisticated psychological levels than was necessary in previous generations. Although underlying psychic processes have always existed in any close relationship, in the past they were often allowed to lie dormant, while today they are not. It does not make the present better or worse; it is simply different. Put in a vulnerable and exposed position, companions are faced with revolutionary changes in the generational life style. These are natural changes, not indications of festering psychic ills, and can be explained by the fact that any human relationship is inherently dynamic.

At the point of emotional crisis for two people, they often feel their relationship is over, and for many today this is true, because external supports are not there to help the union to survive. But it does not have to end that way. A pair can successfully face a substantial transition, one that has become a realistic point of no return, and move through it to more satisfying levels of intimacy. Failure in handling these crucial turning points together means isolation, estrangement and, finally, divorce.

Observing couples in crisis through the years has taught me that there are major turning points for all couples, regardless of socioeconomic status or other variables. They underlie problems presented to a therapist, but are broader in scope than what is explicitly expressed by a couple. Properly called transitions, they are natural moltings of a growing relationship, and can be identified as such.

It is impossible to attach specific reasons—length of the marriage, age or events such as departure of children from home—to these psychic problems. Knowing the particular year of living together that creates the greatest difficulty, or the specific age when life crumbles, would be equivalent to finding a cure for death. Even though all of us have been warned of "the seven-year itch," this symbolic rash can occur in the first, fifth, tenth or twentieth year of living together. Moreover, it usually appears more than once.

Tidy schemes explaining human behavior have only heuristic value, that is, they enable individuals and pairs to define themselves in general terms so that they can discover new directions. They even comfort those who seek some order in their chaos. But they are completely useless for people trying to adjust a delicate and continually shifting relationship—giving their problems labels only makes them feel more boxed in.

What are these universal transitions that determine the direction of intimacy for a couple? They are as follows:

1—Moving beyond romantic love to liking and knowing a mate.
2—Moving beyond disappointment with a partner to acceptance of differences in each other.
3—Moving beyond couple conflict to communication.
4—Moving beyond frustration with a mate to fairness between partners.
5—Moving beyond boredom to self-direction within a relationship.
6—Moving beyond isolation to intimate ties.

For some, passage through these changes creates only a slight ripple in the relationship, but for others, transitions bring violent upheavals. Specific psychic vulnerability to one or more of these turning points depends upon the needs and desires in a relationship.

Transitions frequently—but not always—occur sequentially as presented above. Sometimes they take place unnoticed, are delayed or stalemated, follow a different sequence or cluster together and emerge simultaneously. However distressing these turning points may be, it is possible for couples to move back and forth through them until fulfillment is found.

Twenty years of marriage counseling has taught me, above all, that the hungers of the human heart cannot be denied. They will be fed in one of two ways—either through the enjoyed intimacy of an important relationship or by creating havoc and destruction through substitute satisfactions.

One can make a strong case for attributing all man's and woman's inhumanity to their fellows as a result of faulty relationships in which there is no closeness or enjoyment. The absence of other people who are significant in one's life has led to the downfall and depersonalization of many. This need for others is a continuing hunger and thirst that must be fed and quenched daily if one is to retain one's humanity. We all stand or fall equally in terms of this common need. Hence, at best an intimate tie like marriage is the strongest humanizer and equalizer any of us can experience in life.

A life that is rich in human relationships is not only desirable in itself but can contribute dramatically to physical health. In 1976 anthropologist Sula Benet studied the people of the rugged Caucasus mountains, located between the Caspian and Black seas, who are noted for their longevity. A number of these people live well over a hundred years, an age not considered unusual. How do they do it? The secret, says Benet, is the supreme importance given close family ties and a place of honor for the elderly. They are a generous, nonmaterialistic folk. Wealth is *people* there, and they are valued over everything else.

Contrast this with twentieth-century America. Impersonal urban sprawls are pervasive. Inner-city concrete and steel jungles are the new enemy, replacing the natural foes of man more easily tamed. Careers, mobility and mass transportation often separate us from important personal ties. Divorce is commonplace. Broken lives, abandoned children and crippled financial resources are part of the price we pay for our "progressive" culture. Many citizens feel uprooted in the same manner that their immigrant forefathers were when they first came to this country. Sophisticated displaced-person camps and ghettos exist for the single, the elderly, the divorced and the children of broken homes. They are called apartments, condominiums, planned communities and similar niceties. On top of all this, a strong cult has arisen that lifts the individual to supreme narcissistic importance, seemingly justifying our rootlessness and estrangement from others.

Many look for global answers to the problems of alienation in the United States. Government programs and big-business patronage have not worked. Small examples of grass-roots innovation, such as neighborhoods that adopt each other as family members, have proved effective and continue to work, but these seem only a drop in the bucket.

Other observers are prophets of doom, behaving much like Joe Btfsplk, the scrawny, hook-nosed cartoon character created by Al Capp in "Li'l Abner." Dressed entirely in black, with a dark rain cloud always above his head, his wide-brimmed, crumpled hat is continuously soaked by cloudbursts around him, and wherever he walks, destruction follows. Disciples of Joe Btfsplk say that our traditional source of intimacy, old-fashioned marriage, is dead. We will live in communes, or have several mates, changing them the way we change cars, or enjoy sex with many partners, or never marry. Love and marriage will go the way of the horse and carriage.

Facts support this hopelessness. The mass media have inundated us with reports about the breakdown of family ties: one million links break each year, and younger Americans marry at a later age. Further, sex is no longer reserved for formal bonds; informal living arrangements and casual liaisons make it matter-of-fact. With the demise of the double standard, males and females participate more frequently in passing sex. Modern contraceptives ensure its enjoyment without fear of pregnancy. Even older couples, who missed the sexual revolution, find forays into extramarital involvements more attractive.

Exclusiveness and permanency do not seem a part of today's generation. Companions who enjoy a solid, lasting relationship are shaken by the tremors of change, especially as they see the unions of friends and neighbors collapse. No one is exempt from this pathos; fear has spooked us like corralled horses in a thunderstorm.

Back in the fifties, the last time we were so universally afraid, we built bomb shelters intended to protect us from a hydrogen-bomb holocaust conjured up by the cold war. Should we return to these moldy and deserted refuges?

I don't think so. While all these changes in our mores have taken place, I've been sitting behind closed doors. Sometimes the fallout from social changes has threatened to blow down my doors, but so far I've managed to hold on to my seat.

I have seen innumerable faces and looked inside thousands of marriages. Usually they were faces distorted by pain, hardened with anger, saddened by disappointment or defeated by battle. The couples that parade through my office are a potpourri of America: young mod pairs, old traditionalists, *nouveau riche* achievers, ghetto Puerto Ricans, striving middle-class blacks, closely knit Irish Catholics, Southern plantation families, Main Line Philadelphians, strict pietists, hippie counterculturalists, up-to-date swingers, neighborhood Italian Catholics, homosexual lovers, sophisticated college innocents, staunch military formalists, clannish Jewish realists, blue-collar hard hats, California sun-worshipers, Cuban immigrants and Mid-western farmers.

What do these people say about their bonds? Is marriage dead, as the news media report? Are we all headed for a barren, sterile existence without close ties?

Quite the contrary. Within the intimacy of living together, most couples believe that doom is not imminent. Over and over again, from deep within the human breast, even when the cry is almost drowned out by anger, pain, and misery, I have heard people pleading for a companion to live with, someone with whom to share the future: "I want to be squeezed and reminded I'm human. I want someone close to me who knows I exist as a person."

Lasting monogamy remains the primary source of intimacy for most people. Even those who fail at it remarry eighty percent of the time. Like excited dogs on a chase, people still pursue their dream, regardless of possible failure in achieving it.

Overheated social changes allow people to experiment with varied life styles—communal living, informal arrangements, repeated marriage—but within these differing forms remains the essence of intimacy. Marriage is still the prototype for all expressions of close ties. Rather than succumbing to the general despair, I still see hope for intimate links, even exclusive and permanent ones.

It may seem ironic that a man in the marriage-counseling business for twenty years would conclude confidently that people can maintain significant ties to one another. Consider the fact that daily I see the worst in partners. They bring their rubbish inside my door and leave it behind them. The vindictiveness, anger, pain, hurt, guilt, fear and anguish I see convince me that the slow death of the spirit can be more inhumane than outright murder.

Yet my faith in a couple's ability to find sustaining intimacy remains, even though some people who visit me sever their bonds eventually. How can I remain so sanguine? Certainly, not because my optimism is boundless, but because I have seen positive changes occur in the most hopeless unions imaginable.

When two people want their relationship to work, they will find a way, even though considerable pain and struggle are involved. Their methods of turning around a broken relationship may not be conventional or even provide the happy ending most imagine, yet they will give the pair immense pleasure —an intimacy that has been tested and has survived. In the final analysis it is couples who are determined to work it out that convince me that human intimacy can be found even in today's world.

I feel strongly that the significance of two companions uncovering intimacy for themselves can be as important as any news affecting the course of history.

Continual requests to me from troubled couples seeking help led me to write this book. What guidelines work in a close relationship? What generalizations can be made that provide insight into happiness in living together? What are the practical steps?

From empirical research into hundreds of couples' records, and from my own observations and notes of how partners have solved their problems, I have formulated some suggestions for satisfaction in living together. There is a practical and realistic way for any pair who wish to use this approach to find greater fulfillment in their relationship. Moreover, these methods have been tested and tried with couples again and again, and they work. Further, they have been refined through the feedback of countless people who have used them effectively.

The information gleaned from this research is the content of this book. The manner of presentation comes from the most frequent questions asked. These can be summarized as follows:

First, what is intimacy? People bring many myths, superstitions and distorted attitudes to their union that must be given up if they are to find a measure of closeness.

Second, what are the steps to intimacy? Despite notions to the contrary, closeness does not blossom instantly when two lovers meet. There is a regular progression that leads to lasting intimacy, and these steps can be identified and followed. Contrary to popular belief, these are not the result of hard work and achievement. Rather, intimacy is a happening, an experience that occurs naturally.

Third, how do you keep intimacy once it is found? There are ways to prevent the breakup of any important relationship once the sources of satisfaction have been recognized. Couples can check their bonds to rediscover the roots of their happiness. Establishing guides that work help this process.

I hope that you will find this material useful in answering the questions of intimacy for yourself, and that it will encourage you to enjoy the richest and most rewarding link a man and woman can experience.

I

# What Is Intimacy?

# 1

# Understanding Your Relationship

## *Make Your Expectations Sensible*

THE FACTOR THAT INFLUENCES THE SUCCESS OR FAILURE OF any close relationship more than anything else is satisfaction or dissatisfaction with "expectations." Into that one word are poured all the hopes, dreams, desires, wishes, feelings, passions, fantasies and memories that comprise the meaning of intimacy. Whether it is marriage, living together, love affairs, dating relationships or puppy love, what describes its meaning to any pair is *expectations*.

What do you want from a partner? Love? Companionship? Security? Someone to take out the trash? Pay the bills? Fix gourmet meals? Sex? Understanding? Although these expectations may change as you and your companion change, and as your relationship grows or becomes troubled, they exist throughout the lifetime of any important tie.

These desires are also altered as the world in which we live shifts. Most of us are left breathless by what we see happening around us: contagious divorce, women pursuing careers more frequently than settling for home and hearth, shrinking reasons for family life, couples choosing to remain childless and increased isolation in urban sprawls. Families no longer have the external supports they once had. Relatives, friends, close ties to a small community and even religion do not bolster family life as they have in the past. The results have been disastrous. Like a tree stripped of leaves and branches, the warmly personal relationship between husband and wife has been denuded. With all its warmth and humanness, marriage stands stark naked in the midst of a cold, technological society.

To compensate for these external pulls and pushes that rip partners apart, they have sought more solace and support from each other. But sometimes the cure is worse than the disease. In attempts at emotional survival, people tend to hold on to one another too tightly. Like two frightened children lost in the woods, they threaten to squeeze the life out of each other. Then attempts are often made to escape a suffocating union, and if that doesn't work, they turn on each other viciously.

Any two people beginning or maintaining a love relationship today do so with increased psychological expectations for satisfaction. It is the primary reason for their coming together initially, but it is also the chief perpetrator of problems that occur later. Only when a couple finds an environment in which the two can relax and enjoy themselves does intimacy blossom.

Much of the information available to couples today through the mass media tends unknowingly to reinforce the idealistic or unattainable, and further frustrates their hopes. Rather than contribute to this, I will offer you what I have learned from countless couples who started at the point of hopelessness but who eventually learned that two people can live together with expectations that *work*.

These minimal expectations can be summarized as follows:

1. *A special companion with whom to share the future.* All of us need to know that we are important to someone else. A feeling, glance, touch or expression of affection conveys this continuing interest. The importance each feels for the other is openly acknowledged. Bill J. says it best: "Karen makes me feel like a million dollars when she listens and talks to me. I wouldn't replace her for anything."

2. *An intimate who allows all the moods of living to be shared without censure or fear of reprisal.* This is a definition of companionship, and is far more important than "doing things together." Couples often fail at the latter miserably, but true companionship is simply sharing all the ups and downs to-

gether. Andrea T. expresses this sentiment sensitively: "When we talk together it doesn't matter what we're talking about. It's just nice to know that Kevin is around and we can share something of life together."

3. *A haven from the callousness and competition of the marketplace.* Who doesn't need a warm shoulder to cry on, a person who will allow us to express all the frustrations we collect from interchanges with others? The intimacy of living together gives the opportunity to feel protected, weak or upset—to know that we can collapse into a heap if we wish. Sandra D. says, "I don't know what I would have done if John hadn't stood by me when I was having trouble at work."

4. *Enough abrasion from living closely together to convince us that we are human like everybody else.* Living closely with someone stirs our irritations and stubbornness, but it also reminds us that we are human and have limits. A couple cannot disregard the feelings and needs of each other without doing serious damage to themselves. This is as certain as the law of gravity. Rather than confining us, a close relationship aids the understanding of the limits of personal freedom. Sam B. remarks, "I found I couldn't ignore Betty. When I did, she became upset and I got angry. Things don't work that way. We had to argue our differences first."

5. *A sex life that ages like a good wine.* It takes time to know each other sexually as well as in other ways. To experience the full range of emotions and physical sensations with another requires a prized relationship. Instant sex is possible with anyone, but it remains what the notion implies—a quickie. The full bouquet of sexual intimacy comes only after years, and within the context of important ties. Margaret L. says, "We have learned to enjoy sex in ways we didn't know existed earlier. I wouldn't trade it for the cheap sex thrown around today."

6. *For those who choose marriage and children, immortality through our children.* This still remains an important

expression of a couple's love. Only too aware of the costs, responsibility and involvement necessary, some couples remain childless. This is their decision and should be respected. But there is no substitute for those that wish the enjoyment and trials of parenthood. As Jason V. pointed out, "We waited three years before we had our first child, but it was something we both wanted."

Though subjective in nature, these expectations have to be shared by both partners if they are to work. There must be a balance between the two, with each realizing that they will gradually grow once the rhythms of living together are learned. Even so, even in the best of unions neither person will always receive everything desired. No companion will completely understand the other, not even when that mate is enjoyed and admired to the utmost.

Beginning their shared life with minimal satisfaction, two people can learn to enjoy each other more fully when they become aware of each other's needs. The bonds are weak in the first blush of love; after marriage they wobble. The partners must first learn to crawl together before they can walk, much less run.

Talk your expectations over with your mate. Find out where they are satisfied and where they are unfulfilled. If your relationship is at least minimally satisfying to you both, then it can develop naturally—not by working at it but by having more fun together. A shared starting point is the key to added happiness.

## Develop Strong Reasons for Staying Together

In the waiting room of my office there is a small brochure that describes what marriage counseling can and cannot do. In this brochure I write: "Marriage is the single most irrational act of civilized people." Invariably new clients comment on that remark with disbelief: "That's not true, is it?"

Nothing could be more true. Marriage *is* irrational, and is not based on logic, reason or common sense. It is certainly not a good business deal. It cannot be measured in the way we measure other exchanges between people. In fact, it is an existential leap into the dark for everyone. Think back. Somewhere in the heat of passion, or the passion of heat, you and your partner made a surrealistic commitment to each other to live happily ever after, or at least try to. That is marriage.

It is amazing that of seventy-nine million married Americans today, only two million a year decide to divorce. Sometimes I wonder if it would be wiser to return to the way our grandparents selected mates. Many people groan when they hear me say this. Under such circumstances, at least the benefit of a collective consciousness would be available to us instead of a small single voice saying, "I love you." It sounds very shaky for that voice to say these words, even if the union works more often than not.

We call these passionate feelings that determine our destiny "love," but later we begin to think about our absurd decision. In order to justify it to ourselves we say we married for security, approval, companionship, to prevent loneliness, to get away from home or to fill a void. For some this means that they have combined reason with illogical feeling, and that it works for them. For others it continues to be a puzzle. Sally M. speaks about her troubled relationship: "How could I have been so stupid as to marry him? I saw things in him I didn't like when we were going together, but I thought he'd change."

Unless one can appreciate the irrational in his association, it is highly unlikely that it will succeed. This means considering feelings and valuing them as highly as reason. It is a disaster to talk together as Sam P. did with Fran one day when irritated about money problems. "Let's sit down and talk rationally about our budget," he said with clenched teeth. Neither he nor Fran was feeling logical about it, and both began arguing about their feelings and justifying deeply held attitudes about each other.

Sometimes couples feel that the marriage will be better if they live together first. However, it doesn't necessarily work. People still go through the same emotional expectations in beginning a trial union or informal living arrangement as they do in formal marriage, and they suffer the same grief and sense of failure in breaking up as they do in marriage.

The risk of being hurt remains. There are no shortcuts or free rides in any strong personal involvement, whether it is called marriage or living together. "It crushed me when Thad left," Barbara S. cried. All the strong rationalizations used did not salve the pain she felt when he said it was over. Feelings between companions run deep. Emotions make commitments, even when the brain says something else. The aura of involvement remains bewildering to many.

Accepting the absurdity of our decisions about love with at least a pinch of whimsy is the first step toward understanding. We do not always act rationally, or even in our best interests, when it comes to our union.

Powerful needs and feelings hungering for satisfaction drive us. This recognition, coupled with humor, allows moments of rationality to emerge. When this objectivity is present, we can examine alternatives, uncover hidden parts of ourselves and our partner, and perhaps even find ways to enjoy our mating more fully.

It is in such lucid moments that we recognize that any relationship must be *equally* pleasurable to both if it is to succeed. When one partner has the advantage at the expense of the other (whether intended or not), both will eventually suffer.

No human action can be attributed to a single motive, whether the impulse is altruistic or perverse. Especially in intimate relations, mixed motives are evident. Some are self-seeking and some are self-giving. As a couple allow for both. Discuss the most desirable reasons that brought you together. Do they agree with your feelings, or are they out of sync with them?

Most relationships fail because partners impugn the other's motives: "You just married me to get away from home"; "You couldn't take care of yourself when we married"; "You didn't really love me when we started living together." Or it may be their continuing reasons for staying together: "You don't need me"; "You can't find anyone else"; "You just want security and don't want to have anything to do with me."

Sometimes companions use this ploy on themselves: "I don't feel anyone else would have me"; "I can't love anyone"; "I was on the rebound when I met him." Whatever, all these explanations are unappealing and weaken a bond through loss of respect.

We all laugh when we hear the comedian Rodney Danger-field say of his family, "I don't get no respect." Failures in in-timacy are the result of this type of behavior toward one another, whether or not it is expressed in words.

When I see couples in my office ignoring or name-calling each other, acting spiteful, being defensive or showing disgust for one another in any number of ways, I think of a story at-tributed to an elderly farmer who married the most homely woman in a small, rural town, and when asked why replied, "I didn't want much when I got married, and she was the nearest to nothing I could find." When their association is failing, couples treat each other with the same scorn and sarcasm. Ironically, this usually occurs because the partner is too important for one's emotional survival. Openly admitting your mate's importance to you is the first step in rebuilding a union.

Conversely, when one spouse views the other as unimportant, a show of strength is necessary. Behaving more independently or getting a partner's attention through your finer attributes be-comes the first step in rebuilding a relationship. Even when self-doubts exist, behave with assurance. This is always the first step in strengthening intimate ties.

Given the complexity of human motivation, it is necessary to search for the strongest grounds for staying together. For some, that task is simple, since they met in their love and can easily congratulate one another on his or her good taste. For others, the reasons for staying together are such that they can be used to belittle each other. The latter need to discover the strength of character in their companions to gain respect for one another.

The Irish have a saying: "As good as you are, and as bad as I am, I'm still as good as you are." This feeling creates the necessary environment for a union to survive. Caring, com-panionship, special feelings about a mate and security all work to make couples feel better about staying together. Both must occasionally feel strength and importance in each other for a relationship to sustain itself. They must meet at certain points in their confidence if their bonds are to survive. Find ways of agreement about this that each of you can fully appreciate and admire.

## *Keep Your Eyes on Your Relationship*

There are two ways to view your relationship, each of which gives radically different perspectives. The first gaze is from within, and is colored by one's involvement. It makes companions look entirely different than would a glimpse by others from the outside, since the emotions of a couple are involved.

Fifty years ago the Irish sage George Bernard Shaw sensed this difference when he refused a request to write an essay in a volume on marriage by replying, "No man dare write the truth about marriage while his wife lives. Unless, that is, he hates her, and I don't."

More accurately, no man or woman can be completely objective about his or her spouse while involved with that person. Why? Because once emotionally connected to another person, he or she looks different. The partner becomes a part of one's emotional satisfaction or dissatisfaction, and all appraisals are shaded by this fact.

Many couples overlook this when they employ the second view: looking *outside* a couple's union and commenting on it. From this outlook others are seen, for example, as the "perfect couple," the "odd couple," or a "disastrous marriage." Outside the closed doors of living together partners wear masks and hide their deeper feelings. To pollsters and statisticians they are seen as numbers, pressure groups or partisans in a one-dimensioned manner. But *within* they look different: the perfect twosome is falling apart; the odd couple is enjoying themselves immensely; and the disastrous marriage is full of tenderness and kindness. Appearances remain deceiving to others, and sometimes even to the couples themselves.

When at a cocktail party Harriet E. says, "I don't understand what Pauline sees in Bill—he can be such a bastard," she is not seeing their relationship from within, and doesn't know that Bill acts quite differently with Pauline than he does with others.

From my vantage point as a therapist, I've been able to look at couples from both within and outside. I have seen couples compare themselves to others, either positively or negatively. The results are usually disastrous, similar to the results of looking the wrong way when driving an automobile. Comparison means competition, and couples who do this to each other simply are expressing their inadequacies, or are trying to force their mate to conform to an expected image. It also precludes happiness, since the partner must measure up to an external standard. Troubled pairs are usually guilty of this useless habit and, as a result, come apart.

"Keeping up with the Joneses" means something different in this context. The couple attempting this is envious of other pairs that apparently have captured the secret to happiness, and they are using others to find their rainbow's end. Love will always elude partners who do not find answers within themselves. Always looking over your shoulder and comparing yourself to others can only end in distress. When you're looking the wrong way, accidents do happen more frequently.

The point is that each couple creates its own brand of intimacy, which has the unique flavor of the couple's personalities and of the bond between them. Nothing is more important to a couple than identifying the qualities that make them unique. Being normal is bland and banal. Finding the qualities that each can enjoy in their union, those that make it different and important to them, is a step toward creating more fulfillment in living together.

Take a good look within yourself and within your union. Of course the view will be blurred, since looking at yourselves is like trying to read a newspaper held close to your eyes, but from your intimate position you can still pick out occasional words and phrases that describe your link. What are the qualities you value in your relationship? What are your ways of communicating that make you different as a couple, and that others are not invited to know? Answers to these questions describe the texture of the relationship you enjoy.

## Solve the Puzzles of Intimacy

Any intimate connection between two people poses several enigmas. For their life together to work, couples must piece together a mosaic that allows them to find ways to exist together while feeling vulnerable, living with choices made and fumbling for closeness.

*Feeling vulnerable.* Closeness to another human being necessarily means exposure. It can happen no other way, since intimacy means self-revelation. Naturally, this unprotected state gives rise to fears. To achieve ecstasy, or even enjoyment, one must also experience a frightening anxiety.

Basically this anxiety is related to two different fears: abandonment or rejection, and engulfment or suffocation. To prevent feelings of abandonment some partners grasp for the other emotionally. Bob R. says to Anne, "Since you've found your new career you don't seem interested in me anymore." The fear of losing her is beginning to overshadow their present enjoyment together.

When Anne responds by saying, "You're holding on too tightly," she is fearing suffocation by Bill, and the anxieties of both pervade what once was a satisfying relationship. The result is further misunderstanding, unless the explosive situation is defused by reducing the magnitude of each person's fears.

Every individual struggles for closeness with a companion, yet fears exactly what he or she wants. Nothing highlights this dilemma more than the prospect of formal marriage. In the musical *Camelot* the King sings on the night before his wedding: he anticipates his loyal subject's question "I wonder what the King is doing tonight?" and responds, "I know what the King is doing tonight—he's scared, he's SCARED."

More ashen-faced, trembling people have approached an altar with their mate-to-be than not. Part of the reason for living together out of wedlock is an unwillingness to face the pain of these ominous fears in a legal ceremony that implies permanence. But these fears still strike those who live together. They still are faced with the anxieties as well as the rewards of closeness. Intimacy is simultaneously desired and abhorred by everyone.

Countless couples in my office shout, cry or whine this sentence: "I want to be closer to him (her)," never realizing that they fear what they want, and even sabotage its easy access. A previous history of good experiences with a companion, trusted and tried over time, makes it possible. The risk then becomes worth the reward. However, closeness is impossible for couples who fight or put each other down continuously. They can only reverse this process with time, and through experiences that are light-hearted and fun, where little is risked emotionally. Heavy-handed discussions, carried on ad nauseam, only make matters worse. Begin as infants when you are seeking intimacy. Sit on the floor and play pat-a-cake—both figuratively and literally. Eventually you may learn to share closeness more fully, if you are not shocked senseless by its arrival.

*Living with choices made.* The second enigma of living together is tied to the choices or decisions made that profoundly affect our future. Certainly, selecting a mate fits into this category. Humans are a funny lot in this regard. We worry and dally over our alternatives; for every choice made, we mourn lost options and opportunities not chosen. A simple example will suffice. Have you ever gone to a store, bought some clothes, brought them home, looked them over, and wondered if you made the right choice? Perhaps you picked the wrong color, or could have made the purchase more cheaply at another store, or overlooked a chic style.

Today we have the time, energy and money to do the same with a spouse. Companions are able to leave one another more easily than when previously tied by economic necessities, close-knit families and moral judgments. Even children do not hold couples together today.

"I want to be free," the battle cry of social unrest in the sixties, has seeped into personal relations. Individual freedom is highly prized, and most Americans claim it as a birthright. And the fact is that as a nation we probably enjoy more personal autonomy than any other country in the world today, notwithstanding the CIA, FBI and IRS, for science, technology and added leisure have brought us greater self-determination.

Yet the result is not always desirable. Although people have more choices and alternatives, they are nervous about them, especially when they involve living with another. It is easier to find extra time and resources to worry about our happiness; indeed, some of us make it a full-time hobby. The anxiety created by added opportunities is not always welcomed, even when the advantages are acted upon.

Specifically, it is easier to look for greener pastures when a partner becomes uninteresting. New people met socially or through a career often look more stimulating or appealing. We can act on impulses only dreamed about previously.

No one is delighted by the fact that given the age of marriage and the age of death today, it is possible for couples to live together fifty years. But though permanency and exclusiveness of personal attachment are not valued as highly as they have been, the alternatives are not always appealing, either.

It always amazes me to talk to people who have hastily divorced their mates, and then quickly have jumped into a second marriage. Their old devil is removed, but soon they are visited by new ones created by a complicated relationship with an untried spouse, unhappy children from other marriages, stretched financial resources and similar emotional dissatisfactions with the new mate. Their unhappiness is thereby compounded.

This is not to say that a second choice cannot be better—only that the risk is higher that the same mistake can be made twice. Mourning lost choices is wiser than acting impulsively. At least the possibility must be considered that all the people we didn't marry might bring us more hell than we have now. The freedom to divorce does not ensure happiness.

Part of the problem with having greater freedom and choices is that once the goal attempted is achieved, unhappiness increases. The plain fact is that some people are happier behaving like Walter Mitty, James Thurber's character, who spent his life dreaming fantasies that were never realized. In other words, if you get what you want, be certain that you can embrace it, or at least tolerate it, without damage to your psyche.

Examples are endless. Don C. knew his new love would

bring him happiness when he left Linda, his wife of twenty-six years, for Ann, a younger, attractive companion. But guilt and grief prevented his enjoyment of the new relationship. Commenting on his first marriage, Don said, "It was like cutting off both arms. The children, all our friends, a different life style made it difficult. I even missed Linda. It's crazy. I was a fool." Years passed, and finally Ann left him because their relationship seemed hopeless.

Betty W. desperately wanted a child, and she and George, her husband, tried for ten years to have one. Charts, visits to gynecologists and urologists, intercourse at specific times were all part of their routine. Finally all the effort paid off and a healthy bouncing girl was born. Betty could not understand the horrendous depression, more than the usual post-partum kind, that overcame her. She had what she wanted, didn't she? Or did she? It meant a change of life style for her, one that she had not anticipated. Adjustment to her child took several years, and a readjustment of career ambitions even longer.

Jerry and Sylvia A. wanted economic security. Both worked night and day and achieved their goals: a plump savings account, up-to-date automobiles, a sleek boat and a brand-new house. But instead of enjoying the hard-won fruits of their labor, they bickered over inconsequential problems. The fighting grew uncontrollable, until finally Jerry moved out of their dream house into an empty apartment. Neither understood why it happened, but both were certain that it followed close on the heels of achieving their goals.

Such lessons are important. Recognize that there are two sides to choices. Even when you get what you want, there may be a letdown as other feelings emerge. Consider goals in this manner, with the best knowledge you have of yourself and your partner. Realize that for every decision made, the choices not made will naturally be mourned. Consider your spouse's feelings in the same manner that you consider your own.

*Fumbling for closeness.* The third basic puzzle of intimacy involves the methods partners employ to gain happiness from their relationship. In this regard, couples tend to use the same assumptions and procedures associated with other tasks: success orientation, win-or-lose competition, goal direction, hard work and achievement.

Yet intimacy is never found by such methods. Vickie P. thought she knew how to make her marriage work. Imbued with the Protestant ethic and known as a high achiever, she said, "All you have to do is to try harder and work at it." Her husband, Walter, watched her do it, and this gave Vickie a mental hernia, along with pent-up anger toward her husband, until she realized that is not the way a relationship works.

The cliché runs, "Marriage is a 50–50 proposition." But 50 percent of what? Who keeps score? How do you parcel yourself out? It sounds as if an accountant thought this one up.

There are variations to this theme of vigorous activity to make marriage work. In *The Total Woman* Marabel Morgan tells women to be submissive to their mates, to work hard at making their husbands happy, and offers such suggestions as wrapping their naked bodies in Saran Wrap when greeting their husbands at the front door after work. That's certainly going the second mile in achievement, but what does a woman do after making a fool of herself if her husband doesn't respond —or if he feels forced to respond when not interested?

Even when *both* partners are inordinate achievers and try strenuously, it only confuses the issues. With the best intentions many a pair have worked hard at a relationship, but still divorced—so that they could relax.

When they begin living together every couple should have a set of directions telling them to learn to relax, enjoy and discover one another. Even when problems arise, the first step is to move back to simple fun together. If a union doesn't work on this basis, it won't work by making it more complex. Intimacy is a *natural state*, but people make it unnatural by adding goals, achievements, competition, responsibilities and high emotional expectations. As a result, more frustration and dissatisfaction ensue, and unhappiness is the result.

Couples require a different mind-set to find intimacy than the one used with other goals. The simpler two people can make their union, the more profound and workable it becomes. One person always influences the other, and vice versa. The connection between a pair is always present and partially sustains each of them. Enjoying, sharing and caring are natural outcomes of living with someone you like. Bogged down with other responsibilities, mates do not have to approach their relationship as work. Instead, they can loosen up together and simply appreciate what their companionship brings.

It is this state of mind that works: one that allows both to share the now with the other. Dreams, goals, problems and responsibilities will always be there, separately and collectively, but intimacy is relished *now*. It keeps marriage or any other relationship from being an escape, since each person remains fully responsible for himself or herself. Thus satisfactions through intimacy come more easily.

In short, two share living together, but individually remain totally accountable for their separate fulfillment in life. Living together was never intended to be as deadly serious as so many have made it.

X-rated and open only to adults, under no circumstances should non-adults be admitted to the intimacy of marriage. Chronological age is not an indication of adulthood; only emotional maturity is. In this sense, adulthood comes to people from the ages of twenty to eighty, and for some it never arrives.

Paradoxically, it is only when adults marry that youth can again be appreciated. One of the benefits of living together is that it allows adults a safe return to childhood with another person, so that it can be savored intimately. Adult partners are not forced to continually worry, be responsible or upset, they can enjoy themselves and play together.

Emotionally immature people who marry make their games all too serious because they demand, expect and fight just like youngsters without adult supervision. They have lost the point of living together and fail to reap the rich bounty of two adults sharing companionship.

## Harness the Power of Your Relationship Constructively

Aesop's aphorism "In union there is strength" needs no further validation than it is given by any pair joining forces. Powerful needs—dependency, affection, inclusion, control and sexuality—are entwined in such a way that the whole is far greater than the sum of the two parts. Moreover, the tie brings a third party to every relationship: the *us* part of the synergy that unites *me* and *you*. Sometimes x-ray vision is needed to see it, but *us* exists in equally real terms as *me* and *you*. Rather than two becoming one through their union, as myths about love have it, two become *three*: *me*, *you* and *us*. The synergistic combination of any pair leads to greater energy for both.

This is not simply a theoretical discussion but a practical reality that must be recognized in order to understand any intimate tie. The bond two have with one another sustains them as much as they sustain each other. Once the uniting takes hold in deeper levels of the psyche, the closeness becomes such that neither partner need fear abandonment by the other.

In Uncle Remus' stories, Brer Rabbit came face to face with "de Tar-Baby," a ploy by Brer Fox and Brer Bear to catch Brer Rabbit. When the Tar-Baby refused to talk, Brer Rabbit smacked him in the nose with his right fist. He couldn't pull his hand loose, and then proceeded to get his left hand stuck, both feet and his head in the same way; all were entwined in the Tar-Baby. The more he tried to get away, the more he became ensnared. Finally he was easy prey for Brer Fox and Brer Bear, a captive of his own misguided forcefulness.

The ties of a couple work much the same way. When fought against, they snap back. When accepted and even relished, they work *for* both partners. Divorcing or separating only indicates their strength. Partners threaten to end their relationship over and over again before finally doing so, and then with wrenching pain. The strength of a union cannot be denied; it returns to haunt the duo.

But this power does not have to be menacing, and it can be used by a couple to achieve their fondest wishes. The support and security of closeness often make it easier to face life squarely. Rather than denying companions freedom, it encourages each of them to pursue interests, careers and hobbies. It allows expansive exploration by one's self, yet offers certain knowledge that there is another person who cares. There is nothing strange about the fact that in general married people live longer, have better health and are happier than those who are single.

The secret lies in harnessing this energy to your advantage. In the first place, it is to *your* benefit not to continually fight your partner and end up like Brer Rabbit and the Tar-Baby. Cooperation is always more rewarding than competition.

Secondly, worrying about your relationship wastes energy. Being responsive to yourself and your partner in productive ways saves energy to be used for other purposes. Appreciate the satisfactions of living together and do what is necessary to make it work.

Finally, trust the growth and development of your bonds. These ties usually sustain and increase your mental health. It is a huge relief to know that you do not always have to be accountable, overly concerned or under stress in order to live with another. In this state of mind you can carry out without much effort the necessities involved in living together.

## *Take Your Time in Developing a Relationship*

Relationships have a history, and this must not be forgotten. Some people begin with a thin, one-dimensioned, tinseled picture of marriage, and when it tears, they have nothing left. They understand neither the breadth nor depth of intimacy. Afraid of conflict, pain and struggle, they fail to find the closeness they simultaneously desire and keep at a distance.

W. H. Auden hints at the dimensions of living together in this manner: "Like everything else which is not the involuntary result of fleeting emotion but the creation of time and will, any marriage, happy or unhappy, is infinitely more interesting and significant than any romance, however passionate."

Immaturity blinds people. They do not see past the immediate gratification demanded. Believing the promises of a pop culture that says one can have instant love, or that promises something for nothing, they expect immediate surcease from intense emotional hungers. True intimacy simply doesn't happen that way; it takes time to develop a substantial and lasting relationship.

Just as every human being has a life cycle, so does a couple. Similar to the way an individual develops, a couple goes through transitions that can be identified and successfully handled. This provides grist for the mill in forming an adult relationship. Intimacy can be found at any point along the way, but is much more satisfying once it has been tested.

To use another metaphor, living together is a long and adventurous journey. There are many unexpected alterations of timetables, changes of plans, breakdowns, layovers, moments of peril, disagreements over what to see and where to go, conflicts about the point of the trip, as well as moments of pleasure and discovery. There are no free rides, only companionship. Togetherness is not an escape from living but a quiet oasis. If a person can't make the trek alone, then it is unlikely that he can make it with someone else. No one is forced to take the odyssey of life with someone else; he or she can go it alone. But if one chooses to have a companion, he must realize what's involved.

This requires time. Relationships mature slowly and must be nurtured gently. They march to the tune of a different drummer—different from the one that forces a hectic pace in a competitive world.

Some people are unwilling to stick around to see how the partnership will work. Their threshold of pain is low, and they wish to escape. But starting over with someone new means going through the same process again. This makes no sense— but who said we're all sensible? Like a child who goes to a birthday party bringing a gift and enjoying the games but leaving before the cake and ice cream are served, some people are unwilling to linger long enough with a companion to find gratification of a substantial kind. An increasing number of people like to taste the romance of living together, but fewer and fewer wait around to find intimacy, the best part of living together. Either infatuated with "love" or afraid of closeness, they defeat themselves and their mates in the process.

Take your time and let your relationship grow. Care for it tenderly. Abrasiveness can lead to meaningful exchange, sadness can lead to satisfaction, and alienation can lead to intimate contact, the best part of living together.

## Checking Your Relationship

1. When you started living together, you had expectations about what you would receive from your relationship—the good things that would result from the union. List five of the most important of these; put a plus sign where you feel your relationship is meeting your hopes quite well and a minus sign where you are not satisfied. Compare these with your partner's list. Are there more pluses than minuses? What can you both do to improve the plus side of your relationship?
2. Can each of you easily feel the other's support in actions and words? Are there ways this mutual support can be improved?
3. Since a primary reason for being together is enjoying one another's company, do you still spend time together doing simply that?
4. How has your relationship changed with time? What are the directions you would like to see it move in?
5. Are both of you satisfied with the quality of closeness you share together?
6. Are you able to feel comfortable together at times so that your relationship is not always hard work?
7. Do your good times together encourage you in carrying out responsibilities? Do you still like to please each other?
8. If it is a burden to find time together, then your companionship is not spontaneous and enjoyable. Are there simple ways you can improve the situation?
9. What activities increase your happiness together?
10. What are the special qualities about your relationship that mean the most to you?

# 2

## Doing What Comes Naturally

### Rid Yourself of Excess Baggage

IN THE COURSE OF TALKING TO DISTRESSED COUPLES, I HAVE learned that many people make living together incredibly complex. Caught in the quagmire of conflict, frustration and hopelessness, they complicate the sublime yet simple process of sharing intimacy.

What prevents their happiness? They are unwilling to *give up*. Instead they *hold on* tenaciously.

Males, traditionally, and females, more recently, view living together as an abdication of freedom, but it is not this kind of giving up that I am talking about. In fact, this is a false notion because intimacy brings more freedom than has previously been known. Once the relationship is established, couples are now free to pursue friendships and careers separately and jointly, in ways not known to singles.

Nor is the giving up that I am writing about mean sinking into despair and despondency, or assigning one's destiny to fate. Rather, it is giving up all the constricting attitudes and emotions that will destroy the bond between the pair involved. In other words, it is giving up anything that reduces one's humanity—such negative actions and impulses as:

· Bitter recriminations—they are only returned.
· Preposterous expectations—they are never fulfilled.

- Attempted manipulations and games—generally they backfire.
- Unfounded guilt—it is only reinforced.
- Holding on too tightly—it only makes the other want to leave.
- Responsibility for the other's happiness—it makes both unhappy.

Thus, a good journey together is a process of giving up excess baggage in living. The longer two live as a couple, the more that is discarded. False hopes vaporize. Expectations cease, since what is found becomes enough. Puffed-up superiority is treated lightly. Affected love of inferiority is no longer tolerated. Masks, pretensions and insincere sweetness are dismissed, since they only thwart the fruition of a couple's intimacy. What's left? The bare meat and bones, the authentic feelings of two sharing their existence with one another in all its multivaried forms.

Before this is learned, and possibly even after, shouting is necessary, if for nothing more than to clear the lungs, open the sinuses and let the blood flow more rapidly. In the process, both learn something about the other's affirmation of individuality. With increasing closeness comes understanding, the soothing calm of companionship and the savored pleasure of living together.

The direction necessary in any gratifying relationship is gained by ridding oneself of all the accumulated desires of past dreams.

Consider: What is *not* necessary for your survival as a couple? Travel lighter together by shedding your attempts to change your partner. Save energy by refusing to argue a point into the ground. Refuse responsibility for situations over which you have no control—including the emotions of your mate. Weed out anything superfluous to your union.

Nature abhors a vacuum. Once all the junk from the past is cast aside, something must take its place that is better, or the debris will return. Participate in events that both of you like. Share times of thoughtful conversation. When pain and difficulties occur, don't wallow in them. Keep your view open to enriching experiences by streamlining living together.

## Cure the Primary Malady of
## Living Together: Knots

Many couples tie the knot when they marry and then spend the remainder of their marriage attempting to untie it. Like a child flying a kite for the first time who eagerly anticipates it soaring effortlessly in the wind, only to be disappointed when it never gets off the ground because the string is hopelessly tangled, so companions remain tied in knots.

When couples in trouble arrive at my office, they do so with emotional binds that constrict them. They don't understand their own involvement and feel trapped.

Sue W. wants to be free. John wants to live with her without being rejected. Angie R. wants closeness, but doesn't want to be a slave to Tom. Tom doesn't like the demands she makes on him, but doesn't want to leave. Often they behave like a comedian entangled with a piece of rope who, in trying to extricate himself, succeeds only in becoming more enmeshed.

The task of a marriage counselor is to help people unravel such knots so that they can live together successfully, or else end their relationship when they are unable to live without them. Often partners do not understand how all of this has happened. They start living together with high hopes, but find themselves caught in a net. Not finding the freedom of intimacy and closeness, they feed on alienation and distance.

Knots stifle freedom and choke love, and the process starts simply and innocently. Al C. and Bev F., a young couple in their twenties, liked living together. Both had carefree, fun-loving dispositions, and neither wanted a permanent attachment at that time. Still, they developed knots. On a quiet evening together Al said, "I've been thinking about the future. I want to save money instead of blowing it all the time." Bev didn't like the idea: "Don't spoil our fun now. Let's keep doing as we like." "No," Al answered, "I'm starting a savings account." Bev said nothing.

Several weeks later Bev suggested that they go on a weekend trip to Bermuda. Al refused. After a few moments' hesitation Bev said, "You don't love me anymore, do you?" This opened

Pandora's box, and they spent the remainder of the evening arguing. The result was frustration, misunderstanding, hurt and anger. These negative feelings tied them together in ways not known before—ways that made both uncomfortable.

For many couples the whole gamut of human emotions is played out in the drama of knots: fear is heightened, despair seeps in, tension keeps the knot taut, and guilt and anger create havoc. It is as though the partners were conducting two separate orchestrations on the same theme but with total lack of harmony.

Knots destroy people and togetherness. R. D. Laing expresses this plight in his characteristic way:

> Jack's unhappy that Jill's unhappy
> Jill's unhappy that Jack's unhappy
> that Jill's unhappy that Jack's unhappy
> that Jill's unhappy
> Jill is guilty to be unhappy
> if Jack is unhappy that Jill is unhappy . . .

Living together is being democratic to a fault. Once this can be established between any pair, they have made a giant step toward intimacy. This does not mean that they share equal abilities or duties, but that they have learned to treat one another with respect and trust. Togetherness is basically a cooperative venture, and neither can gain unless each person's desires are considered by the other.

This democratic approach that also serves one's best interests aids in loosening ties so that both can enjoy their union. Learning to live together without chafing ties is the key to intimacy.

## Discover the Direction for Living Together

A definable process based on the flux of the couple's relationship occurs internally and naturally in all unions. Companions in my office fight hellishly one week, then return the following, having aired their lungs, and report improvement. Why?

It happens because people and the links between them never remain static, but move in a positive or negative direction. Gradually—and sometimes not so gradually—a couple's relationship grows and flourishes or else deteriorates and dies. Because of this changing quality there is no such animal as a normal marriage. Boredom and lack of interest between two people indicate that the motion of a relationship is slowing or has stopped, and soon one or both will feel it's over. Whether or not partners are aware of it, spend time trying to keep it going or even understand it, the movement of living together occurs continuously.

The overall flow of most relationships can be traced like a graph of the stock market. Some people like to live dangerously, and their movement is like that of a nonstop roller coaster. For others, it is a boring, straight line constricted by rigidity and formality. Still others find the drift of their marriage like a toboggan running downhill without brakes. Every relationship has dips, curves and rough spots, but in a growth situation the direction is upward, with plateaus along the way.

There are specific qualities to this motion that keep a relationship developing. This insight came to me after watching troubled couples change the direction of their marriage from one that had trapped them in obstinate knots to one that produced loose and flexible bonds enjoyed by both. They had learned to unravel the unyielding knots that kept them shackled to each other. How did they do it?

Talking and listening to Jan and Tom O. offers a good example. A couple in their mid-thirties, married for eleven years with two small children, they first came to see me looking like the shell-shocked victims of a blitzkrieg. Separately they were likable and reasonable; together they were impossible—they engaged in all-out warfare during months of turmoil and pain as they shouted at or blamed and manipulated each other. But gradually all this subsided and, ever so quietly, positive thoughts and feelings about each other emerged which surprised both.

How did this happen? First, each made small attempts to understand each other without defensive retaliation. When understanding remained impossible, they learned at least to tolerate each other's point of view without strong or angry feelings. Next, the encouragement that each felt as a result of the strong sense that the other was trying allowed both to discuss problems without feeling personally attacked—a major milestone for them. At the same time all this was happening, they were urged not to discuss their problems endlessly when at home. They were asked to participate instead in lighthearted activities—an evening out without the children, visiting friends or looking through an old photograph album of their early years as a married couple. Such experiences prompted good feelings together without great emotional risk.

When the turmoil ceased, Jan and Tom began to find a new flow to their union. What they said could only be described as a prescription for positive action that is *simple, easy, direct, sensible, fun* and *inexpensive*. To me, it represents six ways that any couple can use to untie the knots that bind them. Let's examine these methods through their story.

1. *Make the complicated simple.* Jan tried to please Tom by fixing gourmet meals, and when he did not act gracious about her efforts, she blew up. Tom met anger with anger, and usually the shouting would turn into a donnybrook.

Now it was different. She continued to cook, but Tom sometimes did also, and each felt comfortable enough with the other to express not only enjoyment but disappointment about the meals. Jan would fix gourmet meals but did it for herself, not expecting Tom to necessarily enjoy them. By allowing for one another's differences, it became simpler to live together.

2. *Make the difficult easy.* Sex had always been a problem for Jan and Tom. From her point of view it was too mechanical. Tom had to be in the right mood and wanted sex only at particular times, whereas she was more adventuresome and wanted to try new things from the sex manual she had recently purchased. Having sex became a major ordeal; a certain time, place and way were necessary.

Then they decided to relax and approach one another more casually. Multiple orgasms and constant erections were no longer a primary concern. Because they learned pleasure is spontaneous caresses, they could be flexible about the when, where and how of sex. Physical relations almost became secondary to the closeness they shared. Anticipation and the build-up were more important. The direction of their marriage had a new quality. They had made something previously difficult for them easier to manage.

3. *Make the evasive direct.* Jan said, "The most remarkable thing we learned was a way to talk together." Tom nodded his agreement. "We used to assume a lot of things about one another that simply weren't true," she went on. "We were always mind-reading." Tom added, "I never knew what she was thinking about when she was in one of her moods. Now she tells me. It's a relief." Jan continued, "We can fight now without it destroying us, since we don't hold back as before."

Both partners had unknowingly allowed the other to assume a great deal about their personal feelings and attitudes without correcting misconceptions. Therefore each was relying on his or her feverish imagination. The result was misunderstanding, which grew day by day, with increasing tension. To alter this common difficulty they simply had to tell the other what they thought and felt—something so simple that it is often overlooked by many couples. Directness clarifies confusing messages.

4. *Make the dumb sensible.* Tom felt it important to keep his money worries from Jan. It was the "manly" thing to do, since he felt responsible for Jan's well-being, despite the fact that she worked. However, when Jan overspent, Tom figuratively rapped her knuckles. She felt that he was being unfair and depriving, and her resentment zoomed into high gear when she was told to ask him first before buying something. "I'm not your slave. I make money, too, and I'm going to do as I wish," she answered. Tom lashed back: "You don't care if we go bankrupt. You just want to spend without thinking about it." She returned the salvo: "You buy what *you* want, don't you?"

This made their money knot even more taut. How did they untie it? Through simple rules of fairness. It was dumb of Tom to keep his financial problems from Jan, since it only made matters worse. Jan was being irresponsible by not consulting with him about a budget. Furthermore, both had acted on untrue assumptions learned from their parents' marriage. They realized that it was necessary to sit down together and talk about money without attributing selfishness and tightness to each other. Both knew it was absurd to continue fighting about money, and understanding produced a sensible solution.

5. *Make the grim fun.* Due to the gradual erosion of their shared interests over eleven years, Jan and Tom were bored with each other and continuously felt a heavy atmosphere of doom. Marriage was grim and they were imprisoned in it. One of the first steps that helped them change the atmosphere, if not to solve problems, was learning to play together again. Neither wanted expensive amusements since these raised the specter of forcing a good time when they weren't ready for it.

They loosened up by taking walks around the block, treating the kids to a picnic, going to a movie, inviting friends over —nothing elaborate or difficult that would elevate expectations beyond the couple's readiness to handle them. Grimness and tension faded as an occasional smile appeared.

Once the atmosphere changed, they spent evenings sharing long talks. Finally, they approached their differences without duress, and in the process mutually decided that they still liked each other. All this was their warm-up for learning to live together happily. They learned something that many people never do: couples can't live together without a sense of humor. Sullenness vanished.

6. *Make the expensive inexpensive.* Most of us have a heady dose of materialism in our background and equate products of our society—cars, houses, gadgets, clothes—with happiness. However, recently the realization has dawned on us that natural resources are limited, and that much of the consumption of goods today pollutes our atmosphere. Yet most Americans still think that success and happiness must have tangible signs. Jan and Tom were no different; they were not content unless they were full-fledged members of the affluent society.

The problem was their lack of financial resources to maintain their chosen life style. Examining this dilemma, they reasoned that if both worked longer, there would be more money in the till but less time to enjoy it. However, if they didn't work as much, finances would be tighter even though they had more time. It was Catch-22. To resolve this plight, they had gone into enormous debt, and the price of this was continual economic worry and mutual recrimination.

Most people haven't begun to tap their own resources for pleasure, either together or separately, and are dependent on the offerings of society. Tom and Jan changed their views when they realized that a deeper happiness with each other meant less need for possessions, or even for finding companionship in mutual interests. With a little more imagination, appreciation of novelty and creativity they learned that they could play checkers, browse in a crowded shopping center without buying, visit friends and simply enjoy living together. They furnished more of their own entertainment.

Many interests and hobbies were pursued alone. Friends, tennis, macramé, woodwork, crossword puzzles, reading and adult-education courses filled their separate needs, and these activities made each more interesting to the other. Because they increasingly liked being together, they spent less time pursuing something to do. As a result, spending money became less of a problem. They had learned to make the expensive cheap.

There are many Jans and Toms who *sense* this method for untying knots and finding closeness. Although not always implemented, they know it works. Preoccupied with self-created worries or feeling helpless, they wait until a crisis occurs before they take action to alter their relationship. This is not unusual; humans usually wait till pain strikes before changing their behavior.

Crisis is a common experience for all of us. Whether a career decision, physical illness, a troubled child, divorce or an extramarital affair, all of us have suffered emotional upset. But the crisis of intimacy is a special turning point. When two decide they have grown apart, no longer love each other and want to separate, pain is created. But, horrendous as it may be, a crisis does not always have to end disastrously for a couple.

The character in the Chinese language for "crisis" has two

meanings; it is at once a *danger* and an *opportunity*. The danger is obvious, but the opportunity is often overlooked. When two people feel their relationship has ground to a halt, they can do something about it by using the six methods described above.

No matter what the nature of the crisis, or what needs changing, the first action necessary is oiling and greasing the machinery of the couple's bonding. This requires several steps.

First, instead of discussing problems until both are sick of it, be neutral for a time before making impulsive decisions about the future. This means openness to a different direction, even when it looks bleak. Give up hopelessness as much as possible. Neutrality means more choices. Also, it is easier to move from negative feelings to neutrality than it is to change from negative to positive in one fell swoop. A cooling-off period makes this possible.

Secondly, during this fence-sitting period, the couple can spend time re-creating the enjoyment found earlier in their life together—maybe even in the courtship period, with all its awkwardness and impetuousness. Any light-hearted fun or humor shared together can create a different atmosphere.

Thirdly, once neutrality is achieved—and it usually does not occur until a relaxed ambience is found—it is easier to discuss problems. Begin with the least difficult and stay with it until it's solved before moving to more complex matters. Solving the simpler disagreements first creates hope and makes it possible to approach serious matters more confidently. Also, it is easier to chip away at troubles than to tackle them all at once. Couples usually make matters worse when they attempt to solve all their problems in one night.

The safe rule for any couple in crisis, or even one that wants closer ties, is to employ the directions described earlier. Any activity that moves toward simplicity, easiness of approach, directness, common sense, fun or is inexpensive *always* works in attempts to untie knots and find intimacy. Like a finely tuned automobile engine, relationships like these are easier to steer. They purr by themselves, and don't consume the enormous amounts of energy that couples are not willing to give in any case. Almost running themselves, these relationships take partners along for the ride without making a big show of it.

If couples are to appreciate the serenity of living together without being overburdened by anxieties, they must try to find this kind of vehicle and share the driving equally.

The truth of a good relationship's naturalness was graphically brought home to me recently. I was invited to speak to a group of couples high on a tranquil mountaintop. To my astonishment, six of the fifteen couples had been married forty-five to fifty years. It amounted to almost three hundred years of living together! I can't remember when I have been so impressed by a group. Were they freaks of nature? Anomalies of chromosomal mutation? Should they be written up in the *Guinness Book of World Records?* Or were they really the last six couples on earth that would stay married fifty years?

I began to question them, feeling like Ponce de Leon looking for the Fountain of Youth. Were there words of wisdom they could give me similar to the secrets of life of a guru in the Himalayas? "How did you do it?" I asked, treating them with the same awe and curiosity anyone would feel in the presence of celebrities. The first to reply said, "We never really thought it difficult to stay together. You may be impressed by it, but we're not. We had our ups and downs like everyone else." Another voice said, "Children, money and sex all worried us at times. We had our fights and still do. However, we learned to work together." Still another said, "We know how to be kind and respect our partner. It makes things easier even when the bottom is falling out." Someone else chimed in, "We enjoy being together. I'd feel lost without Martha now." A woman spoke up emphatically: "We share our lives and don't worry about what we missed. We don't know why people want so much today."

Then the conversation grew more pointed. "I respect him, even though I don't like some of his traits, and I think he feels the same about me," a woman with sparkling eyes remarked. A laughing voice: "I can't think of anyone who's more fun, even though she's a sourpuss at times."

Deeper feelings emerged. "We don't expect as much from each other as all the young people do today," said a pair speaking almost in unison. The wife continued, "I like Thomas because he's a character and adds more spice to life." A last voice: "We care for each other and have faith in the good Lord to carry us through." It was a sublime and fitting ending to my questions. I must say that initially I was disappointed by these responses. But then I thought about them; had they not confirmed what I already knew? There is a certain simplicity in living together, and when this essence is captured it carries couples a long way. Reading between the lines, I realized that these six couples had learned to make their coupling simple, easy, direct, sensible, fun and inexpensive whenever possible. Through these six steps they had found growth and fulfillment, separately and together.

## Checking Your Relationship

1. Companionship has different meanings for different couples. What are the qualities you find most valuable?
2. Does your union have enough flexibility to provide both closeness and expression of individuality? How can this be improved?
3. Every couple faces difficult problems at times. Can you use any of the six methods described earlier in this chapter to help you find more ease in living together?
4. Can you simplify your relationship in any way so that less psychic energy is needed in everyday living?
5. A test of an emotionally satisfying relationship is found in the fact that couples can enjoy one another in simple and inexpensive ways. Can you still do that together?
6. Couples that are anxious and insecure together tend to make their relationship more complicated. Is there any way you can make yourself and your partner more comfortable together before trying to solve problems?
7. Do you and your partner have nagging grievances against each other that can be cast aside because they are not worth the effort of continuing?
8. Do you have a sense of what is changeable in yourself, your partner and your relationship, and what is not?
9. Can you disagree with your partner without personally attacking him or her, and can your partner do the same with you?
10. What life style fits your tastes? Are you willing to give up what is necessary to achieve this? Is your partner agreeable?

# 3

# Why Love Confuses Intimacy

THE MELODRAMA OF HEIGHTENED CONFLICT IN LIVING together often ends in a crescendo with one partner saying to the other, "I don't love you anymore." This is by far the most frequent complaint I hear about. The collapse of love, prolonged or sudden, sends couples into a tailspin. Hurt, angry and frustrated, they recoil and say the magic words that supposedly end a relationship. But contrary to popular belief and the immortal words of poets, this sentence can signal the *beginning* of a solid bond, one in which intimacy is found.

"Love" is really unnecessary to closeness, since it often hides the real meaning of caring. Tinged with an unreal romanticism, love frequently is vaporous, empty and dreamy, especially when combined with unrealizable hopes or wishes. Like cotton candy, love looks substantial on the outside but melts quickly.

## Ten Reasons Why Romantic Love Confuses Intimacy

I am not an enemy of romantic love. I simply think lack of it has been used as an excuse for many people's unhappiness, regardless of their marital state. It is a nice sentiment, and it makes us all feel good to both express and receive it. But to determine our future solely on the basis of fantasy is sad. Like paramours in a Russian novel, cohorts pursuing it hotly never seem to find each other, or to catch the right train at the same time. This kind of love is unrequited and bittersweet because it exists in a dream world.

1. *"Love" is unrealistic.* A scene with two lovers silhouetted on a beach walking hand in hand into the sunset conveys all the idealism of romantics. It looks good from a distance, but people don't live together that way, except when they are on holiday. Rather, they are at close quarters, where they can see each other's pimples, wrinkles and sags. The romantic vision only separates partners further, since they try to grasp a mirage rather than the real person.

For generations Americans have based their dreams on romantic love. They pay high mortgages in the name of love, sire children and stake their survival on it. In days past, the luxury of idyllic passion was afforable, but today it is hardly possible. Partners must love carefully and sensibly, for the supports from family, friends, church and community are no longer there to stabilize a union when it becomes rocky. Enthusiasts of idealistic sentimentality are soon jolted by the pain of disappointment.

Most of the Western notions about romantic love date back to the Middle Ages. In the courts of knights and kings, troubadours moved freely. The women of the court, including the ladies-in-waiting, were waiting in more ways than one while their spouses were off to the wars. To amuse themselves while their husbands were away, these women became friendly with the serenading troubadours, but high-minded as they were, they wrote precise rules for such liaisons. It was through these extramarital relationships that the ideal of romantic love was first born. From this illicit beginning we developed a whole tradition about extravagantly poetic amour that still persists today. As a result, we marry for love; we divorce because we no longer love; we pine for our lost love; and we ache because we are in love.

The upshot is that many of us blindly jump into amorous interludes without considering the consequences. Even in twentieth-century America, a nation known for its pragmatic genius, people are beguiled by the magic of love. Throwing reason to the wind, our judgment is suspended in moments of timelessness with a lover.

But seeing a companion up close—when our zoom lenses are focused on the known qualities of a partner and a relationship—helps remove the mythical. Then love takes on known realities, and liking, caring and sharing become part of intimate concerns.

Even so, many of us doggedly hold on to our ideal, much like Don Quixote, who dreamed dreams but fought windmills. For some people, beginning a relationship, continuing it for years, or even after ending it, the vision remains, regardless of the partner; the flesh-and-blood mate is never taken seriously because only the fantasy is real to them.

Ralph T. is an example. A charming thirty-six-year-old man married to Marge for eight years, he kept repeating, "I love Marge, but I don't like her." Such statements are absurd. How can one live with someone one doesn't like? People are on safer ground when they like their mates but don't necessarily love them. Then they can find an intimacy that is far better than oceans of love.

The dream must be relinquished in order to enjoy the real thing—intimacy. It's a trade-off. No one can possibly be happy with another person who does not fit the impossible ideal. Dreams can be indulged in as fantasies, larks or pleasurable thoughts, but they cannot be seriously believed or acted upon. Closeness is discovered when two people touch realistically and fondly.

Furthermore, lack of reality in love often places the loved one on a pedestal. It may be flattering to be admired, adored or thought to be perfect, but it also is uncomfortable. Moreover, pedestals are made to be knocked over, either by the worshiper or the one being worshiped.

One fifty-five-year-old man, successful in business and civic affairs and a pillar of his community, told me tearfully after a love affair made public almost destroyed his marriage and reputation, "At least I don't have to live up to an image any longer. All my life I've had to do what others expected. Now I can be myself."

The spouse who elevates a mate wants him or her to fit a picture. Change is sometimes overtly forced. Bob R. said with a mixture of hurt and anger, "I had Gwenn on a pedestal and tried to please her in every way. She did whatever she wished, and I was glad to make her happy. All I wanted was that she love me. Now she says she's tired of me. How could she do that to me? She turned out to be a selfish bitch, and she won't even talk to me when I press the issue."

Finding real love means abandoning the mystique of romantic love. What are the real qualities you enjoy in each other? Hold on to these as a basis of contact for both of you. The here and now can bring pleasant experiences. There is nothing magical, misty or idealistic about the tenderness a couple feel for each other, even if it cannot be contained indefinitely. It can be enjoyed for what it is.

2. *Love expects too much return.* Whether intentionally or not, "love" seduces couples into making serious demands. Jim T. loves Betty and can't understand why she wants to get away. "Why won't he leave me alone?" she says. "He's always after me. I can't do anything without his tagging along, and when I don't feel the same way he does, I feel guilty." They had been living together only six months when their partnership started falling apart, and neither understood how it happened.

True love can't be legislated. Kindness can't be bought. Tenderness can't be manipulated. Caring is given *freely*. Partners must allow space between themselves so that their relationship can breathe. Caring is letting go, not holding on. It is easy to press the life out of another when one makes inordinate demands for affection. Even when such desires are reciprocated, they eventually become smothering for one or both companions.

Danny Kaye, the actor and ambassador to children of the world through the United Nations, tells a touching story about returning home after a lengthy trip. Seeing his young daughter, he wanted to run up, hug and hold her, but she was shy and embarrassed, as many children are when they've been separated from a parent for a while. Sensing this and respecting her feelings, he waited until she was reacquainted with him before giving her that warm hug he needed.

To wait till the time is right is a difficult lesson for some mates to learn. Out of their fears, misdirected hopes or voids in their own childhood, they compulsively seek out another to fill the vacuum in their lives. Unfortunately, it doesn't work. A person who feels hollow usually attracts a companion who also feels empty. In the end both are unfilled, since they simultaneously and frantically try to *receive*, and are unable to *give*.

Although some people claim that they do not expect a return on their investment of love, they are only fooling themselves. There is an undeniable balance in living together, and like the motion of a seesaw, one person alone can't make it work. Giving and receiving is the movement that keeps it going. Martyrdom, embitterment and demands are the prices paid for a one-sided love affair.

To discover whether such personal expectations as caring, tenderness, closeness and communication are being offered by each person, check the balance. Some companions are more adept at giving than receiving, and vice versa. If this equilibrium is satisfying to both, there will be little bickering or frustration.

Learning your own rhythm of giving and receiving as well as that between the two of you allows intimacy to begin. Don't deprive yourself or your partner of either exchange, since it is nourishment for your psyche. Once found, the movement continues naturally, just like the seesaw, and becomes second nature. By learning the rhythm together, a one-sided relationship is prevented.

3. *Love wants ownership.* Most couples know rationally that ownership of each other is not possible in modern intimate relations, but their feelings do not always agree. The more one partner loves the other, the more this sense of vested interest is present. The emotional ties created induce both a desire for control and a sense of jealousy.

To feel special or important to a companion is the wish of most humans. But to be possessive to the point of paranoia is self-defeating. Despite the increase in "swinging" among couples, and more liberal attitudes toward sex outside a relationship, most people are unable to tolerate an "anything goes" attitude adopted by their mates.

Jealousy is not always bad. It is almost instinctual, even though some may call it medieval mentality or original imprinting that needs alteration. Couples have been deceived by a broad-minded rationale that says other sexual liaisons are permissible. Counseling offices are filled with people torn apart by this reasoning.

Sally and Harry L., a young, newly married couple, felt sophisticated in their approach to living together and promised to tell the other if one ever wished more than a friendship with someone of the opposite sex. After several years of marriage Sally told her job-preoccupied husband she was attracted to a man at her office and would like to see him. Harry, feeling both reluctant and threatened, nevertheless thought he couldn't protest and said, "Do as you wish."

Sally indeed did as she wished, and Harry was hurt and depressed. Finally he could no longer tolerate the situation and told Sally that she must choose between him and her boyfriend. When she realized the extent of his anger, she stopped seeing her friend, but both were left confused that their original agreement hadn't worked.

Exclusiveness continues to be deeply desired by most couples, even if it is unconsciously concealed. But the ownership of another on the basis of "love" is neither wanted nor appreciated —as in the case of Carol, who paid the price for possessiveness. Sorrowfully she said, "I always loved Andy. I did all the things I thought best for him. I told him he was too involved with all our friends. He said I was just a suspicious shrew. Why did he leave me for that other woman?"

Unfortunately, Andy was making the same mistake with his new partner as he had with Carol. Because the love between him and Carol had been soured by possessiveness, he was moving on to an untried companion whose sense of ownership was as strong as Carol's. His new relationship was also likely to fail for the same reason.

Ownership in love is self-defeating and wearisome, and it stifles new experience. It quickly obscures the changing faces of intimacy that otherwise would be revealed simply and fascinatingly.

Discuss your expectations regarding exclusive intimacy with your partner. Can you maintain friendships with members of the opposite sex without developing a deep emotional involvement that violates the special relationship with your companion? Most of the flirtation and jealousy that couples exhibit comes from fears of sexual inadequacy, or from the compulsive need to prove oneself as a man or woman.

Bantering or teasing one another about these external threats is the best way to handle them. It is better than ignoring them, or interrogating a partner to discover his or her interest in others. Trust is *not* completely blind; given the circumstances, any faithful mate may make a mistake.

*4. Love wants unconditional acceptance.* "Vickie doesn't understand me," Frank B. shouted as he pounded the desk. Vickie sometimes refused sex or was a reluctant participant. Frank knew she didn't want relations as frequently as he did, but he couldn't tolerate her indifference or lack of desire.

What Frank didn't recognize was that his anger was not primarily about sex. He was expressing his exaggerated expectations to Vickie that she love and accept him unconditionally, and he attached this need to sex. During his thirty-one years he had chosen to satisfy his strong desires for love through physical affection. Scarred by feelings of emotional deprivation during his childhood, he hoped that Vickie would fill his hollowness with all the good things he hadn't received while growing up.

But the empty basket he possessed had a hole in it, and all the warm feelings he received from Vickie kept leaking out. His need for sex was insatiable, and blaming her for being unresponsive or trying to change her only made matters worse. She had her own needs; she too wanted companionable feelings to put in her basket, and felt that Frank was unreasonable.

Somewhere in the deep recesses of our hearts all of us feel that we'll find a partner who will give us everything we've missed in life—the ultimate, intimate admirer—and that the giving will be in the name of love. Unfortunately, it doesn't happen. Love may seduce us to believe that this fantasy will come true, but it never delivers on its promises. The most we can expect is a companion who allows us to share the moods of living together, but who never will provide all the affection we can gobble up.

Frank was forced to take another look. He was not being fair because he expected too much from Vickie. Like other people with voracious emotional appetites, he was unable to appreciate the pleasant times they shared, since he worried about not receiving more. Vickie had enough self-doubts to fall into his trap. Instead of frankly telling him that he expected too much, she became defensive, angry, frustrated and depressed. By her actions, but not her words, she confirmed that she was unresponsive to him, and the result was disaster for both.

Intimacy does not promise that acceptance will come unconditionally. Anyone who believes it does believes a lie. Being misunderstood is a part of living, with or without a confidant. Even when a companion is compassionate and understanding, a degree of nonacceptance always remains between a couple. One of the important signs of maturity is the realization and acceptance of the fact that no one will ever *fully* understand, that everyone is born alone and dies alone.

Can you as a pair enjoy and accept what you have between each other, no matter how imperfect, without always expecting more? Can you tolerate your partner's misunderstanding of you at times without bursting into a machine-gun defense of yourself? And later, after the dust has settled, can you take the time to explain yourself to your mate?

Answers to these questions are keys to perceiving and enjoying intimacy. It is not always necessary to be understood when enjoying moments of closeness. In fact, paradoxically, when those instances of relaxed intimacy are found, more understanding—without words—follows closely.

5. *Love expects you to be a mind reader.* Many forms of mind reading are developed and practiced by couples, but they all are self-defeating. Here are a few samples: "You know I like to go out on Friday night. Why didn't you suggest it?" "I know you don't need me because you always act so self-sufficient." "It spoils it for me when I have to ask, 'Do you love me?' You know I want you to say it without prodding." "I can tell you're angry with me. Go ahead and admit it, you bastard." "You don't love me anymore, do you?"

Call it ESP, lay psychoanalysis, indoor recreation or whatever you wish, but couples are fond of reading thoughts in each other's mind and expect their partner to intuit their moods. This is the specious prerogative of love. It gives some people the right to say: "I'm only telling you this because I love you," or "I'm only telling you this for your own good," or "We know what the other is going to say before we say it," or "If I tell you what I want it spoils it. You know by now what I want."

Deep down, this kind of ventriloquism—that is, speaking for a companion as if he or she were a dummy—is highly offensive. It offends our integrity, love or no love. Yet it is practiced daily. Karen N. greets Bill when he comes home from work and is insulted because he doesn't comment on her new hair style. Instead of asking, "How do you like it?" she expects him to notice it. Bill is equally irritated with Karen because she doesn't see that he's worried about a bad day at the office. Instead of saying something, he remains mum—that is, until dinner, when Karen asks if he would like a second helping. "Dammit," he shouts, "you know I'm on a diet."

All this is done with the license of love. Unless couples learn to be direct with each other about their feelings and desires, communication remains complicated and garbled. Partners stumble and fall over each other's messages. Misunderstanding leads to irritation. Love must not tempt us into believing that mind reading and mind raping are part and parcel of living together.

A pair must give up the nasty habit of assuming feelings, attitudes or qualities about each other. It may be necessary to overexplain your thoughts in order to break the habit, but as long as verbosity is not used as a smokescreen to hide deeper feelings, it works.

Correcting a partner's perception is necessary for you both. Double binds with your companion—when you're damned if you do and damned if you don't in your mate's set opinion of you—are prevented by openness without prejudgment. Allow each person to define himself or herself without speaking for the other. Openness toward each other allows this to happen, and brings the cool relief of intimacy.

6. *Love fosters subservience.* The freedom to weep, a warm place of comfort, a strong hug, giving vent to frustration, all help us feel close to another. But don't be deluded into believing that these signs of humanness mean that one of you is stronger, better or more competent than the other.

Traditionally, males were indoctrinated to protect females. Like Superman, they were expected to scale tall buildings without ripping their leotards, to have a Humphrey Bogart poker face, and to be imbued with the aggressiveness of a Bengal tiger. This macho male image still lingers in most men today, even though cultural changes have occurred.

But this imagery has also created havoc in marriages by setting up a natural imbalance: the strong male and the docile female. Like the Lone Ranger, men were supposed to be strong, quiet and mysterious, and like Tonto, women followed their husbands saying, "Yes, Kemo Sabe." Neither partner really felt like playing these roles, but each was nagged by the feeling that they had to.

From my vantage point of looking inside marriages, spouses never behaved in this stereotyped fashion anyway. Rather, the stereotype resembled the battle of the sexes expressed in the light-hearted lyrics from the musical *Annie Get Your Gun*: "Anything you can do, I can do better. I can do anything better than you." Unfortunately, generally the tone was anything but light-hearted. Wives became nags and covertly controlled the family. Husbands said, "I'm the head of the house," and behaved like stubborn little boys. Love was the glue that held all this together. It taught both spouses to respect their customary roles and made life simpler, if not happier.

All this was drastically changed by the feminist movement, though vestiges of the model remain today. The old, reliable role patterns are gone, and there are endless possibilities for different kinds of intimate ties. But new choices are not always welcome. Couples stand disrobed before one another, stripped of their stereotyped duties. There are a variety of choices: both pursuing careers, conventional male-female roles, househusbands and working wives, sharing domestic tasks, or contracts to decide everything—finances, children, fidelity and even marriage.

Since the foundations of established marriage are shaking, many elevate the promises of love even higher and cling to them. Unfortunately, this often confuses couples only further. To think this is done in the name of intimacy, one can only marvel at how humans complicate everything.

On the brighter side, greater possibilities for ties that are more human exist today than ever before, whether or not couples take advantage of them. Pairs can't be forced through total sex, total love, total intimacy or total joy, or even by being total couples, to find genuine human rapport, but with effort they can gradually find a way together as they explore uncharted waters.

Both males and females must accept the fact that they are human, with similar intellects, needs and emotions. Obvious physical dissimilarities apart, there are no differences between the sexes. Contrasts seen in individuals are due to cultural conditioning and differences in endowment and ability, and not to maleness or femaleness.

The traditional subservience of female to male no longer exists today. Partners may not be equal in talents or tasks, but they are equal in their human needs. Once this is realized and fairness has been established, a pair will enjoy a sense of unity. Have you found this commonality as a couple? Do male and female stereotypes still bother you? Find a way for both of you to feel matched as a twosome, whatever specific role choices are made. This is the foundation for intimacy in living together.

7. *Love expects you to take care of me.* For some persons love is used as an excuse to escape the responsibilities of living. Most people harbor concealed—and sometimes not so hidden—wishes to be cared for completely. Being kept can be enjoyable to dream about, but these fantasies do not come true in real life. Of course, there are ways in which one can make living easier for the other, but when either mate consistently presents himself to the other as frail and helpless, both are heading for trouble. More relationships have been ruined by this imbalance than by any other I know of. When one person chronically gives in to the weakness and powerlessness in the other in the name of love, trouble brews.

This does not mean that a mate cannot be compassionate when adversity strikes. Nor does it suggest that a partner should be abandoned because of terminal cancer. But one spouse can be overly sympathetic, and like the proverbial Jewish mother, serve the other too much chicken soup and poison him. Mental hospitals are filled with people corrupted by love, alcoholics wallow in the affects of tainted love, and marriages are destroyed by people who make emotional cripples of their partner.

The only kind of love that works allows both mates to feel esteemed and important—even if they are handicapped physically or emotionally. Respect must be earned from an intimate, even though it is given willingly. Simply by saying the magic words "I love you," two persons cannot assume that they can misbehave, treat each other any way they wish, or disregard the feelings and needs of the other. Real love is reinforced by positive actions.

Steve A. was forever helping Julie get on her feet. She had debts when they married. A post-partum depression entrapped her following the birth of their first child. She was addicted to barbiturates. Then she found a lover. Steve helped her through all these crises, including finding a way to rid herself of her lover. He thought he was helping her, but what he was doing was killing her with kindness.

Who had more difficulty changing life styles, Steve or Julie? Ironically, it was Steve. He was so accustomed to being the nurse that he didn't know how to behave otherwise. All this helping hid a multitude of confused attitudes, for he had never relished life for himself in a healthily selfish manner. It was a momentous occasion when he gave up his need to help Julie, even though it created nameless fears and anxieties within him.

Likewise, Julie was familiar with her role as the "helpee." Part of the pair's initial attraction had been these complementary needs; a nurse needs a patient, and vice versa. Julie had been treated like a helpless child by her parents, and Steve continued this treatment. When her husband learned to control his need to help, Julie fell flat on her face, but this time she learned to pick herself up. Steve let her do it, but only after considerable inner turmoil, since patience was not his chief virtue. However, in the process she became a more self-confident and likable person, and Steve earned a brand-new respect for himself.

Couples can learn to allow one another room to grow without doing so cruelly. Support, concern, interest and tender bonds can still link them together. Most of all, patience is needed, so that a companion can learn to handle his or her own problems without unnecessary interference. When a mate cares, the strongest support is provided by a few words and a willingness to listen, not by always doing something for the other.

8. *Love refuses to change.* Some companions fight and abhor change. How many partners have said, "Why can't things be like they used to be?" "Why can't we go back to the way we were?" "I want our love to be the same as it was when we started living together." But all the pounding on the doors of time cannot bring back one second of a past period of intimacy. Mates cannot re-create what used to be.

Unless companions live together in the now, they cannot live together at all. Turning points in a relationship occur for all couples as their bonds shift. There are undeniable, unmistakable and unalterable points of no return that each pair must face. But even though they cause pain, they do not have to be frightening or cause panic. Partners can learn to adjust easily to changes, and to appreciate even more the ever-novel experience of living together. Those who look back forget that the present and future may be better.

Pat and Randy Z., a couple married two years, both busy with responsibilities and the challenges of unexplored careers, suddenly realized that their relationship had changed. They no longer felt the warm glow that they had previously enjoyed together. Panic set in. Quick attempts were made to recapture that lost glow, but the feelings simply were not there. Each wanted their union to be the way it had been, but they couldn't force it, and so they grieved over the good times experienced together in the past. The demise of their love seemed like a death.

Hopelessness gave rise to constant bickering and arguments. Sometimes it was finances, at others a lack of interest in sex, but mostly it was one another's foibles—cracking knuckles, chewing on ice, dressing sloppily at home.

Nothing helped, not even attempts at ignoring each other or finding different lovers. Like Linus searching for his security blanket, they sought their misplaced love and affection everywhere. But they couldn't go back, and since they were unwilling to bury the past, they felt their relationship had ended. Neither realized they were going through a transition, and that once they had come out the other side they could develop a new closeness based more realistically on each other's known qualities. First, however, it was necessary to give up their illusions.

Many couples are caught in this bind. They lose hope, imagination and love, never realizing that transitions are not endings, and that new beginnings can follow. Close relationships molt, just as snakes shed skins.

In the midst of mourning a lost element of their love, companions often sound like participants in a soap opera, and can even recognize themselves as part of such a drama. But the drama doesn't have to end like a tear-jerker. Rekindled intimacy can come as described earlier—more simply and easily than most expect—when the couple stops seeking what is dead and gone.

Once Pat and Randy Z. let go of the past, they found the present and learned to enjoy each other again through a variety of experiences. Each took the other at face value, whether sharing a dinner hour with candlelight and roses or a quiet evening reading a book.

Letting go of previous experiences means being open to the present. It allows you to be emotionally available to your mate now, with no attempts to regain a vanished love. Enjoying the present permits a comfortable nostalgia for the old.

9. *Love means I'm always right.* When Martin Luther initiated a revolution that eventually turned against the Holy Catholic Church and became known as the Protestant Reformation, he is reported to have said, "Here I stand. God help me." Many companions make this same statement in one way or another—though without the global implications. Some human

beings have an inordinate need to be right, and they enter a relationship with a bull-headed determination that starts its own revolution.

But living together is a cooperative venture, and there are no right and wrong partners. They are both right in their feelings, or they are both wrong in having come together at all. However, for some people self-esteem is too closely associated with being perfect. They are soon convinced that they are no longer loved because the companion fails to see their infallibility.

Many couples expect me to judge whether they are right or wrong in certain specific contexts. Unfortunately, many of the issues presented to me are matters of personal preference, rather than those that are intrinsically right or wrong. Both partners are right in the way they feel. Feelings cannot be argued; they can only be accepted or rejected. Whether to have steak or chicken for dinner, to stay home or go to a party, to buy a new stereo or keep the old one—these are not matters to be judged by an outsider. How couples *feel* about such issues, and the priorities attached to them, make them right or wrong.

When Mary W. cries, Don gets angry and says, "Don't!" which only makes her want to blubber more. When Don frets about his career, Mary says, "Stop worrying," which only makes him more apprehensive. Feelings are a part of living, and cannot be argued, denied or wished away. The more partners can accept the variety of emotions common to all humans, the stronger their support of each other becomes and the greater self-respect each gains. The more one spouse tries to change the other's feelings, force a partner into a mold, or badger a mate into agreement with his ideas, the less likely it is that this will happen.

Accepting each other's emotions does not mean agreeing with the idea expressed by them. Many pairs don't recognize the distinction. Don W. can accept the fact that Mary feels hurt, even though he doesn't agree with her that he did something to hurt her. Mary can accept the point that Don is anxious over his future without agreeing that his job is in jeopardy. A simple statement like "I'm sorry you feel that way" will often suffice and prevent arguments about feelings.

Partners get in trouble with each other when they don't

separate thinking from feeling, or when they expect one another to agree with their ideas as well as with their feelings. There can be no arguing about the way they feel, but there can be differences between two people in their thinking. Emotions are tied to self-esteem, while opinions can be argued.

There are more urgent considerations in living together than always being right. Expressing understanding of one another's emotions is more consequential than bridging the gap of difference in opinions. Acceptance of how the companion feels—excited, tender, happy, sad, angry, anxious or fearful—is the beginning of psychological equanimity, and it makes possible a wide variety of differences in ideas to exist. Emotional acceptance is a more substantial basis for living together than being morally or factually correct. Love does not give anyone the privilege of saying, "I'm always right."

How important is being right to you? Have you learned to allow your companion his or her feelings, even though you disagree—perhaps even violently—with the opinion expressed? Bonds are strengthened when couples can accept each other's feelings without being threatened.

10. *Love means you must pass all my tests.* Defensive loving says, "Prove that you love me before I risk any of my feelings on you." It wants to be reassured constantly that the partner cares before commitment is made. The most certain way to kill this caring is to continually ask, "Do you love me?"

Such love is seen as something that must be achieved, that exists only when shown and proved continually. Learned in childhood when parents gave or withheld affection on the basis of behavior, it can't be trusted in adulthood any more than it could then. The partner who constantly wants love shown or proven by the mate has never been cared for freely. He or she has paid a price for tenderness, and it is expensive to the psyche. For such a person love means hard work, since it must be earned. Hence, standards are applied to the partner, and both people must dance to this tune of love to stay together.

When the bubble of romantic love bursts for some partners, constant reassurance becomes a chronic necessity. A mate is not allowed angry feelings, differing opinions, other friends or occasional thoughtlessness. Above all, he or she must keep saying "I love you." When one companion fails to pass the tests of love that have been constructed, the other feels unloved and makes an issue of it.

Tim L. was like this with Carol. Their first year together was a delight; Tim was thoughtful and considerate, and showered her with gifts. However, she grew tired of his "overthoughtfulness." She wanted less attention from him and more time to be alone. Tim panicked and was certain that Carol no longer loved him. Like a wounded puppy, he wanted reassurance. "Do you love me?" he asked every day. All she could reply was, "Leave me alone." Compelled by his own need for affection, he pushed harder, and the more he forced the issue, the more she wanted to be left alone. Finally the day came when she could no longer take his insecurity and left him. For Tim it was a self-fulfilling prophecy; he was certain that Carol didn't love him, and eventually she obliged him by leaving.

Tim had to take a hard look at himself. Depressed by the loss of Carol, he grieved for months. How could he live without her? He had to learn that being possessed by "love" never works in living together. Eventually a new understanding of himself and of his own self-worth prevented further obsessions and excesses in caring for another, and he saw he had been deluded in his notion of what love meant.

Real caring for one another can be expressed without the necessity of saying "I love you." When shared spontaneously, the words can be a bonus, but they mean nothing when one behaves in a way contrary to actions that show caring. Trust the overall behavior of one another—that is, all the gestures, thoughtfulness, deeds and words—to convey the caring that leads to intimacy.

These ten reasons why "love" creates problems in a close relationship indicate that it is unnecessary to intimacy. Those people who say they can't love, but are capable of caring deeply, may be more fortunate than those who say they can. Numerous frauds, both knowing and unknowing, have been perpetuated in the name of love, and it is easy to be seduced by its promises despite the immense human suffering that has resulted because of this enticement.

Human closeness comes naturally when it is not confused with or sabotaged by the abstractions of love. When two people come together through kindness, tenderness, liking and caring, they can discover an intimacy that lasts, one that is not buffeted by social changes or challenged by spurious notions. What a couple can feel, touch, taste, hear, and smell together is the basis for enriching closeness.

1. If you and your partner have difficulty verbally defining your love feelings, discuss the ways of expressing love that mean the most to you.

2. Love feelings change and develop with time. Can you describe to each other how these feelings have changed since you first met?

3. What makes you feel certain or uncertain about your partner's caring?

4. Can your love allow expressions of irritation, dissatisfaction and different opinions at times without destroying either one of you?

5. What are the barriers, if any, in either you or your partner to the free expression of love feelings? Can you do anything to lower some of these barriers?

6. Many people feel love means commitment to another. Is this what it means to you?

7. People vary in the importance they attach to expressions of love on special occasions and holidays. Are you and your partner in agreement on this?

8. How are love and sex related for you? Do you and your partner generally agree on the meaning of love and sex?

9. What are the easiest ways you can express love to one another? Are they generally satisfactory to both of you?

10. Do you question your love together? What would help you feel more secure as a couple?

# 4

## Putting Sex in Its Place

SOME PEOPLE MISTAKENLY EQUATE SEX WITH INTIMACY, but they are not at all the same thing, and in fact, they are often quite separate. At times casual coitus can be enjoyed between partners without either enhancing or lessening their closeness, and copulation can be matter-of-fact for two acquaintances not tied together through intimacy. But sex can be most fully enjoyed by intimates, even though it does not always express their closeness.

Thanks to the encouragement of heightened expectations, human beings habitually overrate sex. Generally, actual intercourse lasts only five minutes; more time is given to anticipation, foreplay or afterglow. In the last decade more has been written, discussed, debated and argued about those five minutes than any other period in the life of man and woman. Never before in the history of humankind has so much been expected of so little.

Current literature on sexual functioning tends, both directly and indirectly, to foster greater dreams for physical relations. For many it makes love-making unreasonable. The mate who wishes too much feels that a partner who does not measure up to the performance of a sexual athlete must be lacking. Promises of rapid-fire orgasms and endless ejaculations all tantalize people with dreams of greater enjoyment. But the companion who has never learned the basic pleasures of intimacy in simple and easy ways will never make it to the summit of erotica. A fulfilling bond is not based on performance or demand, but on quiet pleasure shared by two people. Once this lowest common denominator is found, techniques of sensual fondling can be learned, but not until this foundation is firmly established.

Furthermore, many people have ruined their lives by chasing a sexual wil-o'-the-wisp. This natural bodily function, one of several, which is necessary for procreation of the human species apart from the pleasure it brings, has been used and abused to torment decent human beings.

Tal S. said candidly, "I did everything I knew to get sex from Cory, but she refused, or made me wait, or told me to show love first; never was she a willing partner. Finally I found someone else, but I fell in love and almost wrecked my family. It caused Cory excruciating pain and the kids were upset for a long time—all for what started out as 'a piece of ass.'"

Gloria said remorsefully, "Jim turned me on sexually for the first time, something my husband had never done. But it's not worth what I've been through, trying to choose between the two."

## Three Reasons Why Sex Is Never Free

Perhaps it is a result of the sexual revolution, or perhaps it always existed in daydreams, but there is a popular myth prevalent today that says there is plenty of free sex around everywhere. But sex has never been free, even in the most libertine society.

*Sex always costs.* The right to charge is not limited to trollops, bawdy houses and massage parlors. Everyone charges for sex, either openly or intangibly. The cost may be in dollars and cents, or a discomforting bout of gonorrhea or the expense of an evening's entertainment, but there is a price. More costly but less obvious are the intangible outlays. At the minimum, it is an evening's false conversation filled with platitudes. Cathy B. complained, "I like sex with Art L., but he expects me to sit around and listen while he tells me all his troubles, and I just want to go to bed."

Many light encounters with sex leave the partakers with varied feelings of trashiness, shame, guilt, anxiety or urgent desires for more. These are the costs.

More insidious but less understood by partners is the cost of love-making for two people who slide into a relationship because of their passion. Whether novices or betrothed, swinging singles or surreptitious lovers, they confuse sex with intimacy and then find themselves deeply involved with persons with whom they have nothing in common.

Some couples never consider the cost of their liaison, much less the price tag on genuine intimacy. When a man says to his girlfriend, "Let's live together with no strings attached," he is being unrealistic. Psychological ties necessarily involve strings, and when these ties are denied, ignored or wished away, they tend to become knotted.

The sexual revolution may have given us a healthy-minded view of sex and fewer inhibitions about physical contact, but it has also induced miseries.

A college campus is a good place to view the changes wrought by the revolt against sexual restraint. Cohabitation is common, and students who do not grab at the cornucopia of amorous pleasures feel inferior. The norm for sexual experiences has shifted a hundred and eighty degrees in several decades. Although sexual experimentation has always been common, heretofore permissiveness was not openly advocated. Now that it is, students who are ill-equipped to participate are apt to feel that lack of participation is a sign of festering neurosis.

Without questioning the morality of sexual liberation in all its forms, it must be pointed out that the attendant emotional involvement creates upheaval for many. Fragile young-adult egos are not yet shaped. Life in all its experiences is still wonderfully new. The search for knowledge, the development of social skills, the intense idealism, the peripatetic quest for absolutes, the desire for meanings are all—or at least partially—in the minds of even the most crusty young cynics. Add another person to this journey and confusion abounds. As an escape, such a liaison saps energy and hides fears. As a way of life, it stifles growth and personal development.

Through years of counseling college students, I have seen many plunge headlong into a relationship, unaware that sex forces an intimacy that may not be desired, and puts demands on them for closeness that they do not really wish. The average college couple living together spends more time with each other in one day than the typical married couple spends together in a week. They sleep together, eat breakfast and go to class with the other, have lunch as a couple with friends, return to class again, study and dine together, and then return to the sack. Most marriages would not survive this intensity, much less the uninitiated in the rites of love. The upshot is arguments like these:

"I wanted to go to our room, but he wanted me to stay in the library and study with him. He makes me feel guilty for going to the bathroom by myself."

"She gets jealous if I talk to another girl."

"He feels my other interests take too much time away from him."

"Spending so much time together is clammy. It's affected our sex, and I can't even get it up any more."

"He's all over me all the time. Sometimes I just like to cuddle."

"She wants to do everything I do, and never can make decisions on her own."

"I'll be damned if I'm going to pay for our apartment and meals, and he won't even share the cost of my pills."

Would a plea for less involvement be in order, even if it meant less sex? One thing is certain: sexual organs do not atrophy if not exercised daily. More breathing space means room to grow and to find fulfillment through countless avenues. Testing one's resources, abilities and interests would be simpler. Fears could be faced, challenges met, competition understood and limits found. Otherwise, many capacities in a young life are hidden and never fully explored.

Escape into a relationship can be destructive, whether or not it is called marriage. Learning the lessons of living is much more important, even if it is painful. This is not to say that exploring the body to make sure that it works right is unimportant, but to be overly preoccupied with the mechanics of sexual encounters only leads to emotional conflicts that strangle freedom and inhibit growth.

Consider the costs of sex in your relationship. Is your sexual life too expensive emotionally for you, or are you able to operate easily within it? Don't confuse sex with intimacy. Although they can go together occasionally, closeness involves much more. What do you want for yourself?

*Sex regulates life.* No one likes the idea of being controlled in any way, yet all of us are driven to some degree by sexual cravings. Still, though we may feel compelled to find particular outlets, these wishes cannot be satisfied indiscriminately.

Many people have not considered the fact that each of us chooses how to satisfy his or her erotic needs. Will it be through an exclusive relationship? A series of short-lived encounters? Several mates over a lifetime? Casual liaisons? Extramarital relations?

One choice precludes others. Linda C. says, "Warren has to have his cake and eat it too. He doesn't want to give me up, but he doesn't want to give up his lover, either." Warren concedes that this is true, but that he doesn't know how to disentangle himself from the double knots he has created. Enjoying his two liaisons on the same level, the satisfaction is spoiled by the guilt and frustration he feels deep inside, so that neither relationship is fully appreciated.

A person can either choose his manner of sexual fulfillment or leave it to chance. If left to the latter, it will usually create problems not anticipated. The sexual experimentation of the young and their matter-of-fact attitude often make it possible to make wiser choices later if one is not driven wildly by the need for love-making, doesn't attempt the psychically impossible and realizes that sex is *never* free.

*Sex can rob people of intimacy.* Those who see sex as intimacy are never satiated because it is impossible to spend night and day in bed for long. The most that can be expected is experimentation: sex suspended from the dining-room chandelier, or copulation in an airplane restroom at thirty-thousand feet altitude. Anything sexually possible has already been done, and inevitably someone else wants to try it, whether or not he or she is capable of sexual gymnastics.

Such emphasis on intercourse leaves people hollow and un-fulfilled. Jaded and overwrought by the quest for total sex, the searcher often becomes depressed. One such burned-out de-votee said, "I've been to bed with a hundred girls, and I know all the best techniques—they tell me I'm a great lover—but I want something different, and I don't know what it is."

To simply be a connoisseur of sex can preclude knowing one-self and one's partner deeply. Lasting intimacy is elusive, and the innumerable facets of another's personality are never seen, experienced or enjoyed when physical relations are the primary goal.

Of course, enjoyment of a close companion includes grati-fying the desire for sex, but sex is not the pinnacle of intimacy, nor even the most important part of it. When mates find close-ness, physical affection is accepted simply as a part of a pleasur-able relation. But when intimacy is not found, sex often be-comes too important.

## Making the Price Tag on Living Together Less Expensive

Couples begin marriage or living together by looking for answers to personal problems, including their sexual ones. Generally they do not see coupling as a source of difficulty, and that's the way it should be: exuberant hopes, joint goals and tender concerns. But why can't it stay that way?

Most people know that financially it's expensive to live to-gether, and it becomes even more costly if two people marry, buy a house or have children. All these outlays are harassingly present and are continually on their minds. However, couples often do not consider the hidden charges of their cohabitation. This concealed price tag involves the psyche and the price paid for intimacy.

Part of this expense is sex. Just as it costs for singles, so it costs for marrieds. The price may be exorbitant when used like a carrot dangled before the panting spouse, or it may be inexpensive, as when mates touch naturally and easily.

Reduced to two basic attitudes, the price tag for physical relations is either 1) *controlling* and *manipulating* a companion by making sex costly or 2) *caring* and having *concern* for a mate, making sex low-priced.

Controlling means one managing the other to satisfy one's needs. By making threats, provoking guilt, inducing fears, cajoling or inflicting punishment, a partner attempts to force the other mate to do as he or she wishes. Caring, on the other hand, is given freely without expectation of any return, and allows both people to enjoy sex with complete naturalness.

Looking at these attitudes within the context of society it is easy to see that, traditionally, women have withheld sex for love or for other specific rewards. For their part, men have guarded the purse strings and doled out money only for proven needs. Thus were the battle lines drawn in the fight for control, power and dominance.

Today it is different. With more women working, the pay check is less a source of argument, although couples will always disagree over money. Concurrently, once the clouds of repression lifted from women on the subject of love-making, wives began complaining more frequently about husbands as poor lovers. These days both sexes are accused of withholding affection from their mates; this is a common complaint in any marriage counselor's office.

Somehow even today the battle of the sexes is still reduced to sexual behavior. For some it is the beginning, middle and end of living together. For others it is only the beginning, and still others feel it is the beginning of the end. However, for most couples it is a barometer forecasting sleet and snow or bright sunshine. Whatever, not enough attention has been given to the nonsexual meanings attached to physical love, which are more powerful motivators than the physical act itself. For the same couple these meanings can run the whole gamut of human experience at different times: passion, fun, tenderness, relieving tension, expressing dominance, proving one's self, caring, closeness or even spiritual oneness.

Couples seldom consider these nonphysical aspects of sex. The flood of information available today emphasizes the physiology of coitus and techniques to enhance physical pleasure. Pairs tend to view sex from this narrow focus, never considering the quality of their union or the meanings they attach to sex. This approach reinforces a false impression that sex is a purely biological drive that exists outside the context of a caring relationship. Although information on sex as a basic physiological need is invaluable from a scientific point of view, it offends human dignity to consider couples as if they were laboratory specimens.

Sex is highly subjective. The meaning of love-making for a specific couple is based on the quality and longevity of their unique relationship. Both would behave and function differently with other mates. "Impotence" with one companion is not a factor with another; "frigidity" with a spouse is not experienced with another partner. These labels more accurately describe the quality of a particular relationship than the functioning of the individual involved.

Couples who enjoy physical intimacy make it psychically inexpensive for each. Those unwilling or unable to relinquish control pay outrageous prices for sex, and keep their union teetering on the brink of disaster.

What does sex mean to you and your partner? Have you considered the optimum conditions that would allow it to be less expensive for each of you? Since sex masks so many important personal meanings, make it easier for both of you to enjoy it. If you want to disagree about something, argue over the color of the paint in the bedroom rather than your physical pleasuring. Let this one area of life be savored inexpensively.

Find inexpensive answers to these two questions.

What do you charge for sex?
Dissatisfied partners attempt to secure the following kinds of promises from their beloved:

—Undying commitment.
—Showering love in all the ways desired.
—Agreeing to all wishes.
—Never showing anger because of disappointment.
—Continual thoughtfulness.
—Nothing said or left unsaid that hurts one's feelings.

—Change in the partner to conform to one's desires.
—Special treatment at all times.
—Sex whenever desired.
—Willingness to try anything and everything for sexual variation.

Increased expectations like these only guarantee failure, whether or not this is intentionally or subconsciously desired, and create gloom and unhappiness for both partners. Most people who behave this way do so because they have an idealized image of sexual activity. It is difficult for such people to take themselves or their companion at face value, without predilections to make the partner conform to this illusive image. A person who sets such standards has never accepted himself or his spouse realistically.

Those who charge less for sex regard their relationship quite differently:

—Sexual fulfillment for both.
—Pleasing closeness.
—A yes or no to a request for sex each time.
—Enhanced satisfaction in a variety of ways.
—Caring easily for the other.
—Taking each other at face value.
—Spontaneous enjoyment.
—Relaxed sharing.
—Confirming the sexual adequacy of a partner.
—Responsiveness with ease.

These are the least expensive ways to find pleasure together through affection. They provide the basis for intensifying the joy of love-making when two people are willing to begin with few expectations. It should be emphasized that partners must start at the same minimal point.

What does sex cost you?
The unhappy couple pays a royal rate for sex, for it costs:

—Bitching from a partner.
—Feeling put down.
—Feeling sexually inadequate.
—Guilt because of mistreating one's partner.

—Name-calling and unflattering labeling.
—Expenditure of energy.
—Frustration and dissatisfaction.
—Loss of intimacy.
—Tightened knots and binds.
—Continual sexual demands.

Though these costs occur as a result of a partner's attempted manipulation of the other, they boomerang on the one who is making the effort. One cannot enjoy sex at another's expense; it will only end unpleasantly for both. Finding the lowest base of mutual satisfaction together cuts the costs of sex.

This same question can be answered more directly by those who enjoy a good union. The price tag is right:

—Closeness.
—Care and concern.
—Sharing and excitement.
—Tenderness.
—Understanding.
—Relaxation.
—Fairness.
—Risk taking and vulnerability.
—Time to enjoy each other.
—Pleasure for both.

Companions who still play together can ask these questions and enjoy the answers they give and receive. Even couples for whom sex has not been pleasurable can find this exercise enlightening. However, when the cost of sex becomes excessive because of frustration, disappointment, put-downs, guilt and self-doubt, it is wiser to pay in dollars and cents than to endure calamity and duress.

Jim and Brenda D. were married for ten years before they decided to do something about their sexual relationship. The price tag on it was horrendous. Both came from strict, religious families where they had been taught to save sex for marriage. From the beginning they were inhibited and awkward with each other, and over the years they simply compounded their errors. Still, their union had produced two lovely children, a lively eight-year-old boy, and a determined five-year-old girl.

Like many other couples, their honeymoon night had been a disaster. Jim had not made reservations, and it took them an hour to locate a decent motel. Because the romance of their wedding still cast its spell, Brenda wanted the evening to be special. She thought that a quiet candlelight dinner, dancing and a bottle of champagne enjoyed in their room before she slipped into her frilly nightgown would embellish the experience for both of them.

Jim was in a different mood. Although he listened to her pleas, he wanted to go to bed right away; he had waited long enough. Jim won the round but in the process lost Brenda. Sex was painful for her and quick for him that night.

Their first evening was only the beginning of their problems. At times the situation improved, but mostly they lived with disappointed hopes that their sex life would improve. It was never equally enjoyable to either of them; Jim still pursued Brenda, and she was always reluctant, so that neither one was satisfied. Since they were fond of each other in numerous other ways, through the years they tolerated the difficulties. Brenda was a firecracker; she was full of enthusiasm and had a variety of interests besides her husband and children. Jim was a salesman who enjoyed the travel and challenges of his work, but basically he was a family man—when home, he enjoyed playing with the children and sharing companionship with his wife.

An analysis of their price tag on sex revealed that Jim came from a family that rarely showed affection. He felt clumsy with Brenda except in wordless acts of sex, and expected her to sense his real devotion without his saying anything. His most important emotional needs were tied to physical affection. What did he charge? He longed for the day that Brenda would really *want* him. She was too passive and tolerant, and he was never certain that she enjoyed their intimacy.

What was the cost? He felt frustrated and disappointed, but never wished to blame her. It made him sad as he spoke of her, longing for the day when she would respond to his overtures. Although enjoying her and the children made him secure as a husband and father, something was missing: he was unable to turn his wife on sexually.

Brenda came from a closely knit, Italian Catholic family over which her father ruled the roost and vigorously protected his daughters from young studs. Her virginity was secure, but her feelings about her sexual self were not. She was uncertain whether she had orgasm during intercourse, or had even enjoyed the act. Sex, reinforced by Jim's behavior, had cost her much self-doubt.

What did Brenda charge her husband for sex? She wanted an occasional personal word. "Can't you tell me I look nice once in a while, or that you like my eyes, or that you admire my breasts, even though they're small? You say nothing personal to *me*—only things like, 'My skin feels so good when it touches yours.' Ugh! What a turn-off."

In this marriage the cost of sex to Brenda was too high—she continually doubted her sexual adequacy; Jim charged to much —he expected passionate expressions from her that he was really wanted. He overcharged for what he offered, she paid too much for what she received, and both felt cheated and deprived.

How could this process be reversed so that their sexual knot could be untied? The charge and cost had to be favorable to both. Through a series of massage exercises practiced on each other they were able to learn a common basis for sexual pleasuring. After they had mastered this, successful intercourse came more naturally to them because they no longer anticipated frustration or expected automatic performance from each other. Brenda developed a new sense of sexual adequacy for herself simply by not trying to prove it, and she received more tenderness from Jim, both with and without words. Jim gave up some of his inordinate sexual expectations, learned to relax with Brenda and, by not pressuring her to perform, found her more responsive. The manner in which they approached each other became so entirely different—relaxed, passionate and carefree— that it was like a honeymoon, one totally unlike their disastrous one.

As in any other area, in sex the balance of giving and receiving between two people must be fair in order to work. Though it is not always easily found, one starting point is to make the charge and cost of physical intimacy sensible. Each companion is responsible in this regard. Through feedback a pleasurable middle ground can be found. Otherwise, love-making is lopsided, and neither mate will be satisfied. If nothing else works, start paying one another; at least it may create a few laughs that will allow both partners to approach sex more lightly.

## Why Three's a Crowd

Every survey today indicates that couples are having extramarital affairs more frequently, but no one bothers to ask whether they are enjoying them more or less. The old adage "Three's a crowd" is painfully true when there are serious supplemental ties outside an exclusive union. Despite protests to the contrary, an affair does not add to a relationship, make it more interesting or provide more intimacy for the original companions. From my vantage point of looking at outside romances through the eyes of troubled couples, they are the most insidiously tormenting and destructive arrangement any three people can devise—even more than a wrenching divorce.

A love affair is not the same as a chance sexual encounter with a stranger, or even an impulsive one-night stand with a friend. These can be regarded as casual sex, with little long-range effect on a couple. Strong friendships with the opposite sex can also be understood, as long as they are not used to bait the excluded partner, or defended as a constitutional right. But affairs mean important psychic links, and indicate a commitment that becomes intolerable to the initial couple.

Today a new morality expresses itself through informal sex, and its advocates are everywhere. Easy access makes it possible. Both sexes are pursuing careers that involve travel, and even at the office or factory, opportunities exist. Yet even though freewheeling sex sounds exciting, most people are ill-equipped for it. There seems to be no immunity for anyone—temptation can strike even those in high political office or in the clergy.

Part of the attraction is the clandestine nature of an affair, which adds spice to the dull, methodical or empty routine of marital life. It becomes exciting to tempt fate like race-car drivers zooming around a banked track at a hundred and fifty miles an hour, or like skydivers who wait until the last moment to open their parachutes. Like the hard-working citizen who conceals his income so that he needn't pay taxes on it, everyone likes the thought that he or she can get away with something, and an amorous liaison fits nicely into this scheme.

Bliss is also an inducement. In the beginning there are no worries or responsibilities, just sheer enjoyment. For an instant, a day, a weekend, the bills are forgotten, the leaky roof can wait, someone else can care for the children. When a couple is together the hectic pace of everyday living is ignored; carefree, reckless and "in love," the ecstasy of emotion and the orgy of touch are enjoyed in those timeless moments.

Folklore says that an idle mind is the devil's workshop. This adage can be questioned, but it certainly helps to have plenty of extra hours for an affair. From a practical standpoint, it takes free time and tremendous quantities of energy to participate in an amorous interlude. Astonishingly, busy people manage to arrange both opportunities and resources, yet keep a career moving, and even go home in the evening. They plan, hide, deceive, invent ingenious excuses, bluff and weasel their way through situations that the smoothest con man would find difficult. It requires cunning to arrange a rendezvous that remains secret.

But though paramours protest loudly to the contrary, they usually find themselves more intimately involved than they originally intended. It all starts rather naïvely and rationally:

"I want to see you, but I can't make any promises."

"I can't leave my family, so we can only spend time together when I'm free."

"I've never done this before, so I don't know what to expect."

"I'm tired of all the crap I get at home. It's so different when I'm with you."

"How did this happen? I think I'm in love with you."

"Can't we just have fun together and enjoy it?"

At this point the affair seems inexpensive: love for love, with no commitments made. Yet parting is painful, and unreasonable love follows. One lover inevitably becomes jealous or possessive of the other. Anger and guilt are felt toward the spouse or spouses being injured by the intrigue. The emotional consequences, to say nothing of the empty marriage left behind, shatter the nerves of the healthiest sexual athlete. Gargantuan double knots are created by the powerful emotions stirred. Irrationality takes over. Common sense is thrown to the winds. Even when precautions have been taken, mates discover the trysting, and the suffering becomes acute for all concerned. Such liaisons may be tempting, but their cost is certainly enormous.

Intimacy cannot be found deviously. Apart from morality or what family and neighbors think, eventually a liaison brings greater unhappiness than the wretchedness experienced before it began. The best unions cannot withstand the furious emotional trampling that comes with a third-party relationship. Couples simply are not built to share their affections deeply with other persons while remaining together.

Furthermore, affairs violate the simplicity of living together. The only inherent result of extra involvement is more complications and fewer personal satisfactions. Intimacy flourishes for a twosome only when exclusive and aboveboard.

## Six Facts about Affairs That Make Them Costly

The mystery and intrigue of liaisons make them a favorite fictional theme. In reality partners disappear with lovers, or return as different people. They develop new life styles, and discard old values and attitudes. People are profoundly changed by affairs. The outcome is usually unexpected and sometimes shocking.

The puzzles of romantic episodes, coupled with the myths, morality and strong personal biases of people in the couples' social circle, make it difficult to be objective. Still, there are six safe generalizations that can be made. These inferences come from observing the intimate bond through the viewpoint of the couples involved, rather than from that of spectators.

When a couple confronts me with the story of a triangle I feel like a detective attempting to solve a baffling mystery. Mostly the accounts are long, repetitive and painful. Psychically they are costly to the trio involved. Here are the six reasons that make them so.

1. *Partners never have affairs at the same time.* Uncannily, mates decide which partner is to keep their relationship alive. Mostly unconscious, this decision is part of their overall agreement about living together. When one slips into a third-party involvement, the other spouse remains faithful and concerned about the marriage. The loyal partner does not find it psychically possible to enter a surreptitious relationship simultaneously, or even to end the partnership immediately. Later, when the errant mate's trysting ends, the other may take his or her turn—out of revenge, to even the score or to find love. In important ties, the unspoken agreement is that one spouse protects the union while the other frolics.

Laura K. discovered two months ago that Steve had a lover. Arguments, accusations, guilt, hurt and bitterness followed. Laura said, "I've tried everything I know to stop him from seeing that tramp. He won't listen. I even thought of seeing someone myself, but I can't. It makes me sick to think about it. I'm too heartbroken to do anything at this point."

Bill O. felt the same way about Lila. "She won't listen to me. She doesn't care if I kick her out or start seeing someone myself. I told her I was going to, and she told me to go ahead. But I can't do to her what she is doing to me. It would only make things worse."

Why can't people like Laura and Bill do unto their mate as they have been done unto? Emotionally they are caught. This phenomenon is common to any couple in any crisis. If one partner remains strong, the other goes to pieces, whether because of illness, loss of job, a troubled child, separation or financial difficulties. Their marital bonds almost dictate this difference in reaction.

Frequently a family unit unconsciously names an official "worrier." Traditionally, the mother has accepted this responsible role, since managing the home and children has been her task. But now, with more women working and men sharing household tasks, this responsibility is less frequently a function of womanhood.

Every worrier needs someone to worry about, since he or she feels useless unless there is a purpose to be fulfilled. Although couples tend to polarize themselves in these roles, they may switch them from time to time over a variety of issues.

The profound influence one mate has on the other can be illustrated in many ways. Jim and Fran W. were frequent party guests, and usually Jim overdrank and became a bore. Despite Fran's constant protests about his asinine behavior, he continued to drink, sometimes even more when she complained the loudest.

To change the pattern, Fran decided to outdo him at the next party. Feigning drunkenness more than achieving it, she acted recklessly and impulsively. Her behavior had a sobering effect on Jim. He felt protective of Fran, assumed the worrying role and was careful to tell her when she'd had enough.

When a couple polarizes their relationship into rigid roles, affairs are more likely to occur. Usually the climate is created by years of one mate fretting over problems while the other acts carefree. The prototype for such behavior is the devilish, impetuous child with the worried parent. Some never outgrow this pattern and carry it over into adulthood, either in the role of the responsible parent or that of the mischievous child.

Stand-up comics like Abbott and Costello behave the same way: one is straight and the other playful. In an intimate relationship, however, the result is hardly humorous. The partner involved in a liaison knows that the reliable mate is in the background, and so the thrill of a secretive adventure is increased. The playful one wants both mate and lover.

Neither party recognizes that this game is as deadly as Russian roulette until the damage is done. Since *both* spouses are involved in allowing this to happen, one of them can call it off. After months or even years, all three in the triangle grow weary or thoroughly fed up, and want a change. Usually one of the two same-sex competitors ends the relationship (since the third one is caught between the two), but not without enormous grief.

Furthermore, the idea of a third party is often more interesting than the actual paramour. Partners spend months and even years discussing the other person. This ghost eats with them at breakfast, goes along on vacation, joins in intimate conversations, and certainly enters the marital bedroom. The wounded spouse discusses the intrigue as if it was more romantic than what the straying mate has experienced, and only reinforces the lover's attractiveness by continually calling attention to him or her. As if the couple has nothing else to discuss, the mirage predominates. Their life together seems empty without the excitement this creates, even though the stimulation causes anguish.

Often the couple behave like two children, one of whom has withheld a secret. The one with the mystery teases, feels superior or tantalizes the other with bits of information. The friend feels frustrated and putdown, begs to know, threatens, or becomes angry and walks away. This child's game is, of course, much more destructive for adults.

Being flexible about sharing emotional burdens in coupling prevents the easy occurrence of liaisons. For that matter, it curtails other obsessive distractions that emotionally are like a third party. In other words, an affair can also be an absorbing career, an interfering mother-in-law or a pampered child. Once the psychic responsibilities of intimacy are shared, one partner does not have to be cast as the authorized worrier, and the other escape scot-free. Each can attend the needs of the other.

When the scales are tipped in an unfair way for one because of a third party or similar distractions, action is needed to re-establish a balance of power. Ending the relationship is certainly a possibility, but one that people do not choose easily. Short of terminating the union, people think about confrontation, but usually the least effective way of resolving the problem is talk. All the begging, pleading, nagging, demanding and threatening by the loyal companion will have no effect on the other, who has two lovers.

Instead, the straying mate must be *shown* through unpredictable behavior what it means to have a partner who behaves childishly. Provocative action can be taken tongue in cheek without great emotional risk. Examples are easy. Practical jokes like putting cornflakes in the other's side of the bed at night or accidentally tipping over a glass of water on the preoccupied partner at dinner; not being home when the mate returns from a tryst or keeping the straying companion up all night with sexual demands—all make the necessary point of regaining psychological equilibrium between a couple.

Furthermore, such devices serve two purposes. First, they force the fretting spouse out of a fixed, rigid and responsible role; secondly, to the wanderer they mirror his or her own childish behavior. In other words, it shifts the power balance of an unfair relationship. One caution: there should be nothing immoral or illegal in such unpredictable action—simply enough provocation to compel the mate's attention. After this has been accomplished, discussions can take place on an equal footing. But endless exchanges are ineffectual unless the weakened partner has the power to make his point—restoration of the balance of power is required for a new relationship with an intimate companion.

2. *Partners agree to an affair overtly or covertly.* Some people make such statements as:

"If you see someone else, don't let me know about it."

"Maybe having sex with another person will improve our own lives."

"I'd like an open relationship, so that each of us can have other sexual partners without guilt."

"I'll tell you if I'm seeing someone else."

"I can't stand sex, and I know you need it, so find it somewhere else."

"I think you'll enjoy sex more with me if you have an affair."

These declarations are made for a variety of reasons: inferiority as a sex partner, fear of losing a mate, myths about male and female sexuality, hopes for more interest in sex or a wish to prove one's partner unfaithful. When shared, all give relief from personal responsibility for one's behavior. Occasionally they do not do damage, but generally they end tragically. They infringe on exclusive feelings between partners, agitate and wear both of them to a frazzle, and eventually leave them feeling empty and defeated.

Tom and Debbie A. had not had a good sex life in their four years of marriage. "Why can't she understand my needs?" Tom would ask himself in self-pity. Raised to believe that sex was nothing more than a wifely duty, Debbie found little enjoyment in it.

The night that Debbie refused Tom, saying she was tired and had a hectic schedule the next day, a battle started. Tom flew into a rage, and Debbie retaliated by calling him an insensitive animal. "I need sex," pleaded Tom. "Then go out and get it somewhere else," she answered. "Okay, I will," he shouted, knowing that he had many opportunities because of his travels as a salesman.

The next weekend when Tom came home, Debbie was sorting his dirty clothes and came across a shirt with lipstick on the collar. A burst of hurt and rage shook her. "You bastard, what have you been doing?" she yelled at Tom. With tears rushing down her cheeks, she ran into the room where Tom was watching a football game and drinking beer. She shoved the shirt in his face. "But you told me to get it outside," Tom said defensively. "I really didn't mean it and you know that. How *could* you?" *Conflict. Knot.*

Some partners find it impossible to believe that other couples actually agree to affairs, but such agreements are more common than are recognized. However, the agreement frequently is covert. Because of waning interest in one another, spouses develop varying life styles. Surreptitious entanglements snap them back together when they are discovered, but lack of interest between companions cannot be tolerated indefinitely.

Some people feel manipulated or blackmailed by their partners. "Either I live my life the way I wish, or I'm leaving," says the strayer. At first, this may simply mean evenings out, but eventually it may become involvement with someone of the opposite sex. The stay-at-home often feels helpless to do anything about it, since he or she must guard the hearth "because of the children," or because "I can't make it on my own."

Occasionally, a partner is goaded to become unfaithful by the mate's suspicion and jealousy. A certain amount of distrust keeps a partner honest, but taken to extremes it is an invitation to participate in the behavior of which one is accused. To explain every conversation with someone of the opposite sex, to justify time spent away from home and to have to defend the right to enjoy other friends only lead to the desire for the behavior denied.

Collusions that make affairs alluring are common in marriage. Some people build their entire relationship on secret agreements: "You only married me because I was pregnant," or "I loved her when we started living together and hoped she would learn to love me." These arrangements tilt a union from its inception. When partners believe something that makes them feel inferior about themselves, or feel superior to their spouse, the relationship can never achieve equilibrium. Such partial truths, trusted long after the events on which they are based, must be wiped out so that more substantial reasons for staying together can be found.

Intimacy cannot exist between two when inordinate demands for sex are met by seeing paramours, exchanging partners, or having a variety of sexual encounters with others. Sexual activity does not fill emptiness; rather, it tends to make each mate feel more hollow.

Exclusiveness is still necessary to intimacy in a union, since trust and respect are its basis. Anything less violates the very closeness that two people wish.

When derogatory half-truths are believed about a mate, they only fester, and often are used as an excuse to find satisfaction elsewhere. The important and special feelings about a companion that make living together worthwhile must be fostered by both partners.

3. *The injured partner usually can know within twenty-four hours when a serious involvement exists with a third party.* This fact is based on countless observations of the behavior of a mate involved with someone else. Partners may conceal casual sex, but they cannot hide a serious affair. It is implicit in all their actions, whether or not it is picked up by their mates. Why doesn't the aggrieved one acknowledge what is happening? Generally it is denied simply because hurt, depression and confusion follow this painful recognition.

Jim T., a successful banker in his forties, left his wife Estelle abruptly. Although he denied there was another woman, within three hours of his departure Estelle learned the name of the other woman, where she worked, and the fact that the liaison had gone on for two and a half years. Previously, when she had asked Jim whether he was having an affair, he denied it, and she hadn't pressed the issue. Each found it too distressful to openly admit the obvious to the other for all that time.

Denying the possibility of such actions only brings greater grief to a couple. As a topic for discussion it may be distasteful, but it gives a greater sense of reality to a bond, and helps the couple to avoid a folie à deux.

Openness in a relationship means that each mate has a firm grip on reality and sensibly approaches any problem, including the prospect of an affair. It suggests that neither is willing to tolerate a romanticized union at the expense of personal integrity, and that each can face the prospect of bad times as well as good.

Nevertheless, no one needs to be open beyond reason. Even in intimacy, couples require privacy. This does not mean they should be dishonest or disloyal—merely that they keep a portion of themselves unrevealed. Openness and honesty in intimacy do not mean that two people must dump all their thoughts and feelings on each other continuously. Only what is essential for their mutual well-being should be thoroughly aired. Disagreeable subjects should be faced with candor, not postponed indefinitely in the hope that they will disappear.

*4. Partners who have affairs are usually unrealistic about the outcome.* Though many different voices in our land—professional and amateur, sophisticated and uncouth, intellectual and uneducated—state that extramarital relations can be good for a couple, there is little evidence to support this claim. Generally a serious emotional attachment to a third party brings grief to one or more of the persons involved. At best these liaisons have a remote affect upon an intimate relationship; at worst they cause untold misery and waste. The risk is usually not worth the consequences.

Straying companions may be aware that their affairs will be short-lived or futile, yet they will persist in it. Others feel that their hidden love will conquer in the end, just as in the fairy tales enjoyed in childhood. Some, hellbent on proving everyone close to them wrong, behave like Sherman marching through Georgia, leaving destruction and desolation in their wake. But underhanded love relations initiated as a solution to unhappiness almost always end in a tangle of difficult emotional binds, for adulterers do not recognize the other side of their feelings. They see the utter enjoyment and satisfaction of a liaison, but do not anticipate the anguish it will bring not only to them but also to the mate and the lover. Often the delusion of living happily ever after with a new mate blinds one from seeing the nature of the spouse's personality. Even a docile wife or husband can become a vindictive tiger in court. The financial and emotional costs are not recognized when a union is destroyed in this way. Some strayers, successful in careers or other pursuits, develop puffed-up ideas about themselves and think they can do as they wish with impunity. But a tormented companion can easily become vengeful and torture the spouse through relentless harassment —and both can be destroyed in the process.

Unless the adulterer is completely amoral, he or she will feel and suffer the consequences. The actions taken by the deserted mate can even be suicidal, homicidal, or both. Or the strayer may symbolically do away with himself by disappearing, giving away all property, or not providing for the care of the children.

Likewise, he may wish his spouse to destroy him—a form of suicide—by taking everything he owns, shaming him among friends and family and at work, or by refusing him the right to see his offspring. In this process, the deserted partner also ruins herself by seeing her mate devastated.

Unreality is further compounded by a strange sense of obligation:

"I don't want to hurt either my wife or the other woman."

"I can't have sex with my husband, but I enjoy it with Bob."

"I can't decide what to do since my wife has learned about it; I don't want to make a decision and upset either one."

"Even though I broke up with him, I'll always love him more than my husband."

"I feel that I have to marry her since I said I loved her."

A wayward mate doesn't wish to make a decision or hurt anyone, yet knows that the situation is torturing everyone. Easy solutions are not found, indecision paralyzes, and spouses feel trapped. The injured mate alternately feels anger and self-doubt, wants revenge, or desperately clings to the relationship even when it is obvious that it has come to an end. Eventually reality must be faced if sanity is to be restored.

No matter what choice a mate makes between lover and spouse, the first step in untangling the mess is coming to grips with the original relationship. One is never emotionally free to make a second choice until the first mate is confronted with the truth of one's feelings. This may mean ending a relationship painfully, but it must be done in order to make a real beginning with someone new. Otherwise, the first relationship remains repressed and will return to haunt the partner attempting escape.

Intimacy is never available to someone who is unable to face grief and pain, or who is unwilling to risk ending a relationship with a cherished mate. This is the inevitable risk of closeness.

5. *All three parties involved feel cheated about the outcome.* A triangle means a competitive situation, since three is *always* a crowd. Since they all cannot have each other, emotional conflict is inevitable, and since no decision is fully acceptable to all, a no-win situation is created. In the end, the excruciating pain experienced is sometimes worse than the grief of death. Further, the uselessness of it all eventually becomes obvious. For some, it takes months; for others, years.

The straying mate returning to the injured spouse feels defeated or grief-stricken. The hurt companion shares this misery, since he or she feels the other lover is preferred. The straying mate who leaves feels guilty. Often this prevents enjoying the new partner, who likewise feels that he or she is getting only a partial mate, and who also bears the onus of breaking up a marriage.

Many people neither recognize nor acknowledge how these powerful feelings affect them, though they always reveal the effects in some manner. A respected clergyman, feeling compelled to marry his mistress, left his wife of nineteen years, gave up his career, received a quick divorce in the Dominican Republic, married his sweetheart and moved to a different state to start anew. Two years later he remarked to his ex-wife, "I'm still not happy, though I thought this would make me so." Contentment is not gained by tearing apart the past.

Sometimes there is a different twist to the outcome: the hurt spouse, after the straying mate returns, decides that he or she isn't worth keeping. Such statements as "I only have a shell of a husband now," or "I don't love her anymore," are common. There is no easy solution to these knots, but the pain can be minimized by being frank with the original partner.

Giving up the unreal dream of managing a triangle is part of finding satisfying closeness. The notion that intimacy can be found illicitly is a contradiction in terms. The most that can be expected is an interim love affair. Authentic closeness must come in the warm sunlight of open affection, not hidden from others.

6. *The couple's relationship is unalterably changed.* The months or years of struggle when deciding the outcome of a union take its toll. More often than not, couples get back together. From my clinical observations, there is a 70 percent chance of this occurring, even after many separations and tumultuous reunitings. In the other 30 percent of cases, the straying partner marries the paramour only half the time. At least as often he or she finds an entirely new companion who has not been involved in the web.

When original partners are reunited they generally find their relationship empty—there is no love and a great deal of mistrust. Their confidence in each other is shaken, and despair prevails. The battle may be over, but the war is lost. It is difficult to regain satisfying feelings toward each other because both are scarred from their struggles. If the relationship continues, it is because the mates find a renewed basis for coming together. If they decide they still care for or like each other, they have a foundation for intimacy. Otherwise, the same behavior will occur again, or there will be a divorce.

Surprisingly, many couples have survived a triangle problem and made their relationship work again. The testing may nearly destroy the union, but it also can shock both back to their senses.

Companions who stay together do so because they recognize that the struggles of the past have taught them something. An unknown mate brings new conflicts; at least with their original companions they know what they have—even though it is not always appreciated—and minimal caring for each other remains. In the long run scars from the past do not mar the present. Both learn to be forthright and to trust one another. A degree of immunity from recurrences of this pattern is established if each mate insists on a sensible agreement about the future. Intimacy can still be developed by two people, even after their partnership has been shaken by an affair.

## Checking Your Relationship

1. What are some of the meanings you and your partner attach to sex?
2. How important is sex to you as an expression of intimacy?
3. What are your feelings about exclusiveness in your sexual relationship?
4. If sex has created problems for you and your partner, can you find a mutually satisfying starting point to build a more enjoyable relationship?
5. Since variety in sex is a matter of personal preference, do you and your mate generally agree on your preferences? How can this be better understood between you?
6. Is there still fun in your sexual relationship for both of you? If not, how can you improve the situation?
7. Can you freely say yes or no to your partner in sex without creating strained emotional feelings?
8. Do you view yourself as a good lover? How can you both improve your individual image?
9. Can sex still be exciting and spontaneous for you at times? When it is not, does it bother you, or can you accept it matter-of-factly?
10. Has your sexual relationship improved with time, or has it become stale? What can you both do to make it more interesting to each of you?

# 5

## Your Needs Are Legitimate

### Make All Your Desires Valid

MANY ADULTS RECALL WITH NOSTALGIA THE PARENTAL mistreatment they endured as a child and the common fantasy they indulged in, which goes something like this: "If I died, Mom and Dad would feel really bad about all the wrong things they've done to me. Boy, one of these days they're going to feel sorry."

This delicious thought satifies a child's primitive sense of justice, for it redresses the balance in the natural war between the big guys (parents) versus the little guys (kids). We come by sympathy for the underdog naturally.

Another universal illusion of childhood is doubting one's parentage. "Are these two people I live with really my father and mother, or did they adopt me? How can I ever know if I'm theirs? Maybe the hospital made a mistake and gave them the wrong child." Needless to say, this befuddlement is compounded when a parent goes through several marriages, and the youngster has a series of stepparents and stepbrothers or stepsisters.

Such feelings natural to childhood cease to be enchanting when maintained as adults. Yet, surprising as it may seem, many have bastardized themselves just as surely as children do. We meet them every day on the street, at work, and, unfortunately, at home. These are people who have failed to legitimize those wishes common to all humans: a sense of belonging and security, a desire for recognition, a wish to care and be cared for, and a search for new experiences in living.

Of course, such "bastards" do not make good intimate companions, for they have learned through misplaced parental promptings, faulty socialization and defective relationships that they should not receive what they want emotionally to satisfy themselves. They use stealth, subterfuge, force, manipulation, machination, deception, self-righteousness and masked questions to gain a semblance of fulfillment for themselves. The means used often undermines their ability to find the very intimacy they desire.

For these misbegotten companions who treat themselves with little care or respect, life is filled with responsibilities, idealized images to follow, anxieties and insatiable desires for approval. Living together, or even alone, is filled with shoulds, oughts, and musts. Nothing comforts one who has bastardized himself, for satisfaction in living is always around the corner, or will follow once a goal is achieved, but is never in the *now*.

All human beings are legitimate. Their feelings and wishes make them so. Illegitimacy comes only to those who do not openly acknowledge their longings to themselves or to their companions. Hidden or blocked needs between two people surface like an air-filled beach ball held under water and then released. These needs cannot be disavowed or wished away; inevitably, they only reemerge as frustration, anger, guilt or pain. Every need and wish we have, no matter how inconsequential, is legitimate; to believe anything less is to refute one's humanity. This does not mean that these desires will always be satisfied, either by oneself or by one's companion, but nevertheless they remain valid.

The more one finds gratification for his or her needs directly, either through self-fulfillment or within the context of intimacy, the greater the likelihood of happiness. Unsatisfied inner needs lead to most of the mental and psychosomatic ills that plague people today.

All forms of psychotherapy are dedicated to the primary purpose of helping people to legitimize their feelings and wishes so that they may live more satisfyingly. Anything that either partner in a relationship can do to help this to happen enhances intimacy for both.

## Learn to Assess Your Wants and Wishes

Closeness requires transparency about one's desires. For someone who has not admitted these wishes to himself, much less to a companion, frustration and conflict are the certain result. Secretly finding satisfaction for yourself, or battling with a mate over your right to fulfill yourself is self-indulgence of the worst kind.

Many couples waste enormous quantities of psychic energy clashing with each other, never remembering what they originally wanted, or what they intended to happen. Under duress, or within the climate of conflict, the specter of a displeased spouse looms, and so defensiveness, bitterness and attempts to justify censured behavior are the order of the day. How much simpler it is to say, "What do I want for myself and from you?" Guarded partners can never have a satisfactory union because they live tangentially with one another, always keeping an eye on what the mate is doing, or gauging whether he or she will be displeased with any new action initiated. Like two Japanese wrestlers, such couples forever encircle one another attempting to find a hold that will give them the upper hand, but unlike the wrestlers, they can keep this up for years with few time-outs. Sensitive to one another's moves, they are always reacting; they keep track of real or imagined offenses, and are eager to even the score. Sheer exhaustion usually sends them into a therapist's office to discover what has happened, and why living together is so complicated and fatiguing.

Once a time-out is called, each partner can discover what he or she wishes, and even learn to pursue desired personal goals. But this cannot take place as long as a partner is seen as the epitome of evil or as a barrier to one's fulfillment. People who are unhappy with themselves easily blame others—especially a close companion—for their miseries. Living together thus masks the real point of living. Defensive anger and blame furnish the only excitement to those who have aborted their private needs and aspirations. In other words, an individual may argue incessantly with a mate in order to escape responsibility.

"What do I want?" is a question that partners need to ask separately and jointly over and over again. Not only does it cool the heat of battle, but it has several other positive effects. Confusion can be cleared up; responsibility for pursuing one's destiny is assumed; differences between mates are recognized and accepted; preferences are determined and weighed in importance; nonessentials are cast aside. Knowing what each of them wants helps couples decide how they can live together without sacrificing the basic wishes of either one.

But "What do I want?" is not always easily answered. Many respond to this query negatively: "I just want peace and quiet"; "I don't want to be bothered"; "I just want the arguing to stop." Others think in global terms: "I want to be happy," or "I want everything to work out."

Good answers to the question are more likely to be found in modest responses: "I'd like us to have an enjoyable dinner together without hassle"; "I'd like to walk around the block together once in a while"; "I'd like to play tennis with my friends without feeling guilty." More ambitious responses concern pursuing a desired career, developing a life style compatible with one's values, finding avenues for self-expression, and exploring the meaning of companionship for each spouse.

Ask this question freely and repeatedly without fear of selfishness or reprisal. Admit deep yearnings and longings. It is the only way to find intimacy together. Partners often don't realize this, for it sounds self-seeking and contrary to the spirit of living together. This simply is not so; your wants and needs serve to clarify the differences between two people and give alternatives to each of you. Impulsive escapes from each other no longer become necessary, and other destructive actions between mates are curtailed. Through practicing the healthy art of selfishness, couples can consider their decisions with less heat and more light.

A young couple in their twenties, living together for two years, found themselves chasing each other in circles. Tony H., an accomplished artist already successful in his career, was not satisfied with his relationship with Chris L. Though busy with friends, college and a career in teaching, she, too, was unhappy. Pursuing separate interests offered some relief, but both felt they were missing something in their life together.

Rather than confronting their desires for closeness directly, they made excuses to themselves, were defensive and argued constantly. Continually explaining their actions became boring to each of them. It would be easy to separate, but they remembered their previous good times together, and each of them still cared. Neither wanted to be alone, but they had not discovered how to be together successfully once the romance of courtship had faded.

Chris thought Tony held on to her too tightly through emotional demands, and she often felt defeated by his greater adeptness in arguments. To counter his control, she was elusive with him, spent little time in their apartment, and acted provocatively with other men in order to gain self-approval as a woman. Naturally, Tony became jealous, mistrustful and more possessive, and most of their time together was spent arguing about her possible involvement with others. These free-for-alls prevented a relaxed look at what they wanted for their relationship; neither was able to stop the round robin.

Easily seduced into arguments and confusion, Chris and Tony took weeks to reduce the muddle in their minds and to spell out their respective wishes. Both had to stop overreacting to each other and take a serious look at their separate and joint desires. Eventually, as priorities were sorted out, differences were discussed and common hopes were voiced, they decided that their separate and joint needs were not mutually exclusive. However, this was effected only over a period of time as they found new pleasurable experiences with one another, and tested ways that brought satisfaction to each. When they were able to keep their desires in the forefront, there was no need to retreat to savage child's play.

Healthy selfishness prevents overreaction. When confusion, frustration and painful disagreement exist, the first step out of the morass is to decide what one wants. When this is shared with a mate who is reacting in the same way, misunderstanding can be minimized and camaraderie found. Though this approach may seem contrary to togetherness, it clarifies what partners are arguing about and determines whether they can satisfy each other. When they are caught in the whirlwind of chronic conflict, it is the only way to find a semblance of sanity.

"What do I want?" sounds like an easy question, but it is fraught with all the responsibilities and consequences of self-knowledge. It helps a couple discover intimacy individually, an intimacy that deepens and ripens with time.

## Recognize that All Your Feelings Are Important

Close proximity in any living arrangement means friction. For intimate companions this abrasion can be minimized by recognizing that all the feelings between a pair are important. At one time or another, most couples have felt that their disagreements were silly or stupid. The exact opposite is true. *Nothing* that happens between a man and woman is psychically unimportant.

"Why did we quarrel over who left the glass in the den?" "Why did we get so angry about the car being dirty?" "I shouldn't have been angry because you were five minutes late." "It was silly to be furious about your misplacing my comb." Such comments between mates indicate they feel foolish about their irrationality. Apparently these couples do not realize that they are not arguing over the glass, the car, the five-minute wait or the missing comb. Rather, they are disagreeing because their feelings were not acknowledged or their needs were unsatisfied. These trivial arguments furnish the excuse to express their conflict of feelings and needs. The real culprits in these incidents are the lost feelings of respect, thoughtfulness and caring. The argument can cease once one partner acknowledges the other's feelings with a simple statement like "I'm sorry you feel that way," even though he or she may not see the validity of the disagreement. Unless ruffled feelings are acknowledged, all the defensive justification, retaliation and nit-picking or the like that follows will not cure the situation. This process is simple yet magically effective; a couple often need do nothing more to alter a situation than to sincerely and openly accept the feelings of the wounded one.

If this step is not taken, disagreement can escalate into feelings of rejection and hurt. These feelings are more difficult to acknowledge or accept in one another, and usually lead to all-out war. People have separated or divorced for much less than a messy car or a lost comb.

Conflicts magnify in proportion to each partner's unwillingness to accept the feelings of the other, and over a period of time will destroy the intimacy any two may have together. All the common problems that attend aborted closeness—boredom, arguments over personality traits, sexual difficulty, threatened separation—fill the vacuum created by the absence of intimacy, and the two original lovers become enemies.

Every message a mate conveys in words to a partner is accompanied by a feeling. That emotion may be fear or anger, joy or tenderness, bewilderment or anxiety—or any other feeling in the vast range of human emotions.

These feelings are acknowledged subliminally, if not overtly. Disapproval of the other's feelings is also conveyed in the same manner. Communication breaks down because feelings are unacknowledged, even though thoughts are understood. Marshall McLuhan's axiom "The medium is the message," indicating the withering significance of written language and the heavy reliance on electronics, such as television, can be restated in interpersonal terms. Often in intimacy the feeling is the message, and is paramount over the spoken word.

Some, with poor self-images, rely too heavily upon their partners' acceptance of them for feelings of personal worth. As a result, they often feel helpless. In a conflict more time is spent by such a partner in seeking approval than in giving any positive feedback to the other.

Mutual acceptance of feelings and needs help both to tolerate misunderstanding. Marathon discussions and arguments that couples continue into the wee hours of the morning only prove the futility of trying to gain total acceptance from each other. At times each companion must be willing to endure nonacceptance.

Feelings, however negative, do not have to be justified, analyzed, denied or explained. Mutual acceptance of feelings has a profound influence upon the quality of a couple's closeness. It is the bridge that unites two dissimilar humans, so that each may walk across it to touch the other. Nothing can be more important for a couple than allowing the full range of human emotions to emerge and be accepted within the context of their intimacy.

## Learn to Be Kind to Yourself and Your Partner

It's amazing that so many people live with the self-image they set up for themselves years ago: "I've always had an inferiority complex"; "I've been insecure all my life"; "I've always felt I could do anything I wanted"; "I'm a perfectionist and have to do things just right"; "I'm a worrier and always will be."

Whether their self-images are positive or negative, people tend to treat themselves as though they were case histories in psychology textbooks. And often an intimate companion tends to reinforce these outdated designations.

Can you take that image of yourself out for a moment, dust it off, and reexamine it? Self-worth is not a static concept. It fluctuates as one goes through life, depending on circumstances that give rise to feelings that are good and happy or bad and self-destructive. It is self-defeating to maintain a fixed view of oneself because it denies the possibility not only of change but also of growth.

In an intimate relationship, it is necessary to inform a partner about one's varying states of mind to prevent recurring misunderstanding or erroneous labeling. A mate can sense confident or worthless feelings in the other, but doesn't always know the origin of these feelings. Short-sighted spouses tend to think that each is the prime cause of the other's good or bad mental health. This is *never* true.

Positive feelings of self-worth are related to career fulfillment, favorable experiences with other family members and friends, and good fortune with particular interests, as well as to happiness with a companion. Moving close to a partner only emphasizes preexisting moods based on these other experiences in living. Being kind to oneself or to a partner means consideration and calm acceptance of these fluctuations in self-esteem.

When a mate is irascible or depressed, it makes the other uncomfortable, but unless the condition is pathological, the distressing mood will pass as naturally as it came. Trying to argue a partner out of a mood, blaming oneself for his or her problems, panicking, being overly sympathetic or persistently giving advice not only are useless but often make matters worse.

Quiet acceptance of the other's feelings of worthlessness or bruised self-regard allows them to pass more quickly. There is nothing a partner can do to alter the situation except to express concern. That is the best form of kindness.

Mike O. can't understand Kim's unwillingness to visit friends when she's tired and has had an upsetting day with the kids. He assures her that going out will make her feel better. She says she prefers to stay home and relax quietly but he can go if he wishes. He says he will stay and be with her, even though she protests that she would rather be alone. Helpful Mike tries to force her to talk when she doesn't want to and ends up arguing. Rebuffed, he pouts the evening out and refuses Kim's affectionate advances in bed. The next morning both greet the day stolidly with only a few words of icy politeness.

When an individual's self-worth is confident and vital, he or she is more likely to be generous and considerate with a mate. Such feelings are contagious and the mate will respond in kind. Some partners cannot tolerate a mate's good spirits when they themselves feel unhappy or depressed. So they often succeed in dragging the other down to their level and eventually begin to feel better about themselves long before the partner recovers. Such partnerships never seem to allow both the right to feel cheerful simultaneously. Knowing when to leave the other alone can be an act of generosity.

Being kind to oneself and a companion allows both to profit from the union. Even though a couple may begin a relationship with impaired or tattered self-esteem, the therapy of togetherness can strengthen the sense of self-worth so that both feel more confident about facing life.

Crippled self-esteem for either of the partners is an enemy to both. A pair can overcome the debilitating effects of diminished self-worth when they have learned to trust themselves with each other. Trust is earned through repeated instances of mutual support. Bolstering each other's self-esteem is beneficial to both when accomplished genuinely.

This does not mean automatic acceptance of all personality traits or all forms of behavior. It means championing in the other what is stable, authentic and is based on proven trustworthy behavior. And it also means challenging questionable areas realistically even at the risk of angering the other.

Michelle P. had dreamed of returning to school, and now the time had come. For years she had wanted a career in the business world, but twenty-two years of marriage and four time-consuming children had held her back. Jason, a prosperous architect, encouraged her in her new life—he had not forgotten the years she had helped him through school. But he was not ready for the ambivalence shown by his wife when he tried to keep her in her studies. Although she accepted his financial and emotional encouragement, she resented his patronizing attitude. Several blasts by Michelle brought him back to earth. Thereafter support was more humbly given and gladly welcomed. Her new sense of self-esteem eventually brought both increased satisfactions.

Self-worth can be measured daily by partners according to their values of success and failure in living. If the synergy between two people is right, the assessment will be known by both and will support their quest for happiness. Nothing needs to be hidden between a man and woman sharing their journey through life.

Being kind to yourself and your partner makes both living and togetherness easier. This does not necessarily mean generosity in purely materialistic terms, although, of course, an extravagant present or trip is always a treat.

Schooling oneself in self-charity is not as easy as fantasizing about it. One must learn to take self-appreciation in small doses before enormous gulps of pleasure can be swallowed.

Many a self-effacing companion has choked on abundant good times looking for the necessary suffering in the situation.

## Save Up Your Self-Pity for Fifteen Minutes a Day

First learned in early childhood when we experienced parental injustice, self-pity is an emotion known to all of us. Part of learning to be kind to oneself is compassion for the child that still exists within one's adult frame. But this sympathy should stop short of total indulgence of the self-pitying self.

A common malady for those who fail to achieve intimacy with another, self-pity can become a chronic habit. Some have developed the habit along with involuntary psychic and physical ills. In fact, all of us, at one time or another, have called the office to say we have a cold, upset stomach or whatever—instead of saying, "I want time off to lick my psychic wounds."

Self-pity can be consciously controlled, whereas psychic ills, such as anxiety attacks and depressions, cannot, because they are involuntary. But with both emotional and physical illnesses, heaping copious amounts of self-pity on them will further incapacitate the patient.

Norman Cousins tells a fascinating story about his bout with a serious collagen disease, an illness involving connective tissue. Chances were one in five hundred for his recovery from this disease that completely cripples and brings unrelenting pain. He had every right to steadfastly bathe in self-pity. Instead, with the permission of his physician, he developed his own treatment plan: massive doses of *laughter* and vitamin C. Both were designed to reverse the physical effects of the disease, based on scientific studies he knew about. And they worked, whether they were primarily placebo or intrinsically valid. They prevented his complete physical breakdown. Although Cousins said nothing about self-pity, there must have been moments of self-indulgent despair that were curbed through his use of laughter (supposedly beneficial to his body chemistry), stimulated by reading humor encyclopedias and watching old "Candid Camera" classics.

Some people are not as successful in checking self-indulgent feelings. They habitually complain or, like Chicken Little, see the world caving in only because a piece of it fell on them.

Often, when intimacy is threatened, especially through the possibilities of separation or divorce, self-pity becomes the dominant emotion. In a crisis situation partners often feel immobilized and helpless; the clouds of self-pity easily roll in and obscure a couple's communication.

These feelings are best kept in check or discussed with a therapist. But for those unable to resist the pleasures of self-pity, a designated time each day can be used for the purpose of enjoying them. Fifteen minutes, to be exact, when one can retreat into one's bedroom. There the floodgates can be opened, tears can fall like waterfalls, and woes can be recounted freely over and over. To make the effect more satisfying, sackcloth and ashes—the symbols of lament and mourning in biblical times—can be added. (A piece of burlap could be draped over one's shoulders and ashes from the fireplace sprinkled on one's head.) Refreshed from this catharsis, one can come out of his retreat, ready to face life squarely.

## Checking Your Relationship

1. Do you and your partner generally agree on your life style together?
2. Are you both able to share your feelings with each other in an open way even when they are not pleasant?
3. Being kind to yourself in numerous ways that satisfy your desires is important to your well-being and the strength of your union. Can you do this without feeling selfish and without it being detrimental to your relationship?
4. Are you both basically satisfied with your relationship? What makes it work for you? In what ways could it be improved?
5. Can you and your partner affirm your personal rights without undue anger or guilt?
6. Are you and your partner able to reveal your strengths and weaknesses without undue embarrassment or fear?
7. If you both argue too much, it means something in each of you is unsatisfied. Can you both discuss ways to find more happiness together?
8. Do you find yourself too preoccupied with how things will be in the future? What can you enjoy separately and together *now*?
9. What experiences for you and your partner provide closeness? Can these be encouraged by both of you?
10. Do you pout, feel self-pity or get angry when you don't get your way with your mate? Are there better ways to handle these feelings so they do not interfere with everyday living?

# 6

# How to Feel Equal to Your Partner

DESPITE ALL THAT HAS BEEN ACCOMPLISHED BY THE women's movement, the sexes remain unequal. Males and females still *look* different if nothing else, even though there are predictions of an androgynous strain or unisex human, smacking strongly of characters in George Orwell's 1984.

Moreover, with all due respect to our founding fathers, it must be said that all men (and women) are not created equal. Different socioeconomic backgrounds, talents, abilities and levels of intelligence make people—both male and female—unequal.

However, in intimacy at least, equality can appear if both partners fully recognize that men and women are the same in their needs and feelings. Emotional equality is the basis for commonality between companions. Someone very wise said: "Don't walk in front of me, I may not follow. Don't walk behind me, I may not lead. Walk beside me and just be my friend."

## Change Your Position Without Losing Your Balance

If you have been accustomed to walking behind, in front of, or, in addition, looking down or up to your companion, intimacy is difficult to find. Start all over, and try walking alongside your partner.

People that live together, whether or not they are married, often confuse egalitarianism with division of household labor, career priorities and the shared responsibility of child rearing. There is no way these tasks can be divided precisely, even with the legal acumen of a corporation lawyer. Emotional equality is not based on written contracts about who does the washing or who walks the dog. Couples who have tried this procedure have found it doesn't work.

At least, feminists have helped remove labels. There are no longer stickers on brooms, dishes, food, vacuum cleaners and children saying, "To be handled by women only." Likewise, lawnmowers and tools are no longer for men only. All tasks and responsibilities in living together are up for whoever can and wants to handle them.

Confusion about roles and obligations is often created by all the old myths, parental cues, perfectionist attitudes, and responsibilities associated with marriage and family living. Often notions about dependability, duty, obligations and loyalty are either embraced stoically or disavowed vehemently. Partners often compete over who is the more responsible:

"I pay the bills, and you never know how much money we're spending."

"I've spent more time cleaning the house than you. All you do is sit on your ass."

"Why can't you help out more with the children? You never do anything with them."

"I'm tired of working and taking care of the apartment. Can't you do a damn thing?"

"Why do I always have to tell you what needs to be done around here? Can't you see?"

"I do all the cleaning, cooking, and washing and you never appreciate it."

"Why can't you phone our friends once in a while and invite them over. How come I always do that?"

"You never call anyone when things break down. Why do I always have to do it?"

Endless complaints continue when partners have not learned to consider each other's feelings. They must realize that tasks in living together will never be shared exactly; they cannot be weighed on the scales of justice and meted out in equal portions. It makes more sense to take the practical view and allow for differences in ability: one companion may be more adept at financial matters, another at organizing household routines, and still another at following through on details.

If anything really needs doing, someone will do it. If one is hungry, someone will cook a meal; if a bill needs paying, someone will pay it. If one is bothered by a messy room, someone will clean it; if clothes are soiled, someone will wash them. That someone may do it because he or she was trained that way, because it bothers him not to have it done, or because he or she can't force the companion to do it. For whatever reason, individuals tend to do what is necessary for their own mental health. All the complaining, pushing and screaming are unnecessary and waste precious psychic energy.

Most of the so-called "responsibilities" in living together are products of parental imprinting, personal idiosyncrasies and attempts to be like someone admired. Living together can be relatively simple when not encumbered with priorities unessential for living. Nor will a simplified life make one a hippie, or a dropout from society, unless one wants to become one.

If a couple made a list of all the various duties they consider important, and removed from that list only what is necessary for survival, 10 percent of the list would remain. Henry Thoreau proved at Walden Pond that simple living can be good. But living together can be as complex as a couple chooses, so long as there is agreement on the life style.

## Since Anyone Can Be a Bully or a Martyr, Give It Up

Those unprepared for emotional equality unwittingly make one of two basic mistakes that are obnoxious to a partner. Either they become bullies whose word is law or they become martyrs and feel victimized. Both forms of behavior effectively repudiate shared human needs and feelings, making attempts at intimacy difficult.

Bullies condescend, patronize or vehemently pressure their partners, while martyrs deny legitimacy to their own personal feelings, provoke guilt through self-effacement or grovel and swear allegiance to the partners' best interests. Neither approach to intimacy sounds appealing, but numerous couples are caught behaving this way, even when they dislike seeing such behavior in themselves.

Why do people act this way when they know it works against them? Because they have either bastardized their feelings and needs, learned surreptitious ways to satisfy their desires or are afraid to risk exposing their feelings. Openness to risk and vulnerability is always present in two people who enjoy each other.

Jim T. says to Ginny, "You never clean the apartment. It's like a pigsty. Why the hell don't you do something around here?" That kind of statement masks Jim's real desire for recognition from his companion; he is saying, "It makes me feel you care when the apartment is clean." Unless this emotion is eventually revealed directly by Jim, Ginny will continue feeling he is an insensitive bully. Later, discussing whether they should go dancing that evening or stay home, Ginny feels rebuked by Jim's refusal to go out and she cries, "You take advantage of me, and I let you, but you never want to do anything I want." Jim feels guilty for hurting her feelings, but also thinks she complains and whines too much. She is on her way to martydrom unless she can alter her approach.

These brief interchanges do little damage to a pair unless they are continually *repeated* and both feel defeated by the other—then Ginny will be sure that Jim is a bully, and he will be convinced that she has become a martyr. Thereafter they will approach each other automatically expecting anger, guilt, refusal or frustration. No flexible or open communication is possible, since the manner of approach to each other is always stubbornly the same.

To untie their knot, first on the agenda was not talking about why they behaved as they did, but finding a way to approach each other from a position of equality, one that did not imply superiority or inferiority.

In order to accomplish this, each first concentrated on personal priorities, inviting the other to join in events mutually shared. Ginny learned not to be defeated by Jim's unwillingness to participate in her favorite activities. She either enjoyed them by herself or with friends. Jim learned from her behavior that he couldn't bully her into doing what he wanted. He was forced to admit his feelings and needs in a gentle way in order to have her respond. Through this process both discovered an approach to each other that was equitable, and they recognized for the first time that the other's happiness benefited each personally.

At times couples need to make a show of strength with one another to prevent faulty communication. The maxim "Actions speak louder than words" is especially true when a companion is caught in an arrogant or a subordinate stance. Both positions are self-defeating, as well as detrimental to intimacy.

Each must learn to stand on his or her own feet to effectively prevent a lopsided relationship. Both need only a moment's reflection to recognize that when each is satisfied, their relationship will not only survive but grow stronger.

## Reach Across to Touch, Not Up or Down

When the feelings and needs of one's partner are not acknowledged on a par with one's own, *both* must pay the consequences, which can be dismal indeed. The lord and master will have a depressed wife; the controlling spouse, a drunken companion. The partner of a perfect person may say, "I'm not good enough to stay with you, I'm leaving."

Because companions receive what they give, it is to their own advantage to treat their mates fairly. Emotional equality is an essential basis for the practical realities of living together. But countless couples are unaware of this important truth. A husband thinks he is better than his wife because he is president of a company and she is "only" a homemaker. A woman feels superior to her partner because she earns more money. One companion expects special treatment from the other because he does so much work around the house. All this does not mean psychological equality.

What equality in the home does mean is that each takes the

other at face value, accepting all feelings as legitimate and important for both. Specifically, it means that the husband's disappointment and frustration about his failure to receive a career promotion are no more or less important than the wife's distress over her broken vacuum cleaner. Nor is his sorrow any more or less important than his daughter's similar feelings about her broken toy. In short, emotional equality considers the feeling and not the event. Cultural values assigning certain individuals greater prestige than others do not apply within an intimate relationship.

Thus reaching *across* to touch a companion, not up or down, is both poetic and practical. It is the very essence of intimacy. The feeling of equality is a necessary ingredient for any union that is deeply human. It acknowledges ones worth simply because one exists. Nothing is required to earn it, since it is the birthright of every individual.

## Learn to Be Number One in Your Relationship

Everyone wants to be number one. It's the American dream. In business, politics or sports, being *numero uno* carries with it recognition and tremendous rewards.

The glamour of being number one is especially dramatic in sports. After the game is over, the victors are besieged by worshipful fans and by television network crews. Occasionally an outstanding member of the losing team may be interviewed, and the comment always runs like this: "We'll have to work harder next year to win. It's the only thing that's important. Being number two is nothing; being champions is everything."

Numerous couples have brought this competitive spirit into their relationship. A partner may decide that he or she is not only second but sometimes third, fourth, fifth or even tenth in relation to the mate. The arena has moved into the home, where it can be just as bloody.

The "inferior" mate sees himself or herself as outranked by parents, children, friends, organizations, the partner's career and the partner's ex-partners. Trying harder does not move such people up in the standings, as it has for Avis. It simply makes them more angry, bitter and hurt.

People in this predicament have a distorted perspective and rarely find fulfillment. They fail to see that an intimate relationship is the only place where both must be number one, or both will find nothing together.

How can two be number one simultaneously? There are several ways this can occur:

*Stop comparing yourself with others.* All of us have felt second to someone else at various points in life. Maybe it was because a parent preferred a sister or brother, or another sibling was always served the biggest portion of cake at the dinner table, or someone else dated the person we wanted to take to the high school prom, or we didn't get into a prestigious college, or someone else got the job we wanted. Everyone knows the put-down feeling of being number two.

In contrast, the early romance of living together makes us feel special and important to our companion—a number one, no less—and for some, in a manner they have never experienced before. But this feeling can subside when other realities enter the picture—a career, relatives, children, ex-spouses, friends or even the cherished memory of a deceased mate.

Because some wish to hold on to that special feeling of being first, they are jealous or envious of other interests and people in the partner's life. They see the partner's evening out with friends of the same sex as a threat, a conversation with a co-worker of the opposite sex as a rebuff, a displayed picture of a parent in the living room as disloyalty and a forgotten valentine card as proof they no longer count.

Most assuredly, the challenge of one's career, and the time spent pursuing it, can be devastating to the partner who is inclined to measure his or her position in one's life against one's external involvements. "Your job is more important than I am," says the wife—and more frequently today, the husband —who feels displaced in the partner's affections.

This type of comparison becomes treacherous. A forgotten anniversary causes wounded feelings; a talk with an ex-spouse indicates divided loyalties. Working overtime can bring the same reaction, and so can dancing with others at a party.

Attempts to reason with the aggrieved partner are futile. Defensiveness and justification make the accused seem more guilty and provoke tirades. The situation doesn't improve when a "downgraded" partner tries harder to be number one, because the effort itself cancels out the feeling of being first.

Then what does work? Changing the focus of a couple's communications from meaningless comparisons to an emphasis on shared pleasurable experiences always helps. When times together are not spent in argument and frustration, they can be uniquely enjoyable. Each can still tell the other about actions that cause displeasure, but will do so without sounding hysterical. If both still care, efforts will be made to please the other. But more important, each must believe in his or her basic lovability, so that threats imposed by external events or involvements do not become destructive.

*Share special times together.* Modest acts of kindness work: an unexpected invitation to lunch together, a telephone call to say hello, an expression of concern, an affectionate touch, a compassionate look. And after an exhausting session of arguing, a present of a wilted rose might help.

Grand designs rarely work when two people feel estranged from each other. Teresa and Ed H. were apart much of their eight married years together. Ed, a driven man, spent considerable time traveling as a manufacturer's representative. Teresa, a professional realtor, had a broad range of interests and friends that kept her satisfied, but still she yearned for his special companionship. When home, Ed usually retreated to his favorite recliner and sat glassy-eyed watching the tube. She wanted more than a limp, overworked zombie. When Teresa began threatening divorce, both agreed they needed a mini-vacation to get reacquainted.

Preparations were made for four days at the beach. Ed would meet her there after he finished the following week's travels. Fortunately, they both enjoyed the sun and ocean, and fishing from a nearby pier. A hand line and eighty cents' worth of bait had given them many hours of fun together.

On the last day Ed impulsively decided to charter a deep-sea fishing boat. Teresa agreed to go, even though she was doubtful that she could stomach a whole day at sea. Copious provisions of food and beer were purchased for their adventure, and sunrise departure ensured a full day's pleasure.

Unfortunately, a southwesterly blew in while they were at sea. It was still midmorning, and although Teresa grew increasingly nauseated from the choppy waters, she refused to tell her husband to turn back—it pleased her too much to see him being active instead of being perpetually inert. Ed sensed her discomfort, but said nothing. Both were apprehensive as the ocean grew rougher. The captain said this was only a minor storm and it was moving rapidly, so they did not have to turn back unless they wanted to. Since he did not make the decision for them, they were forced to make it for themselves—something neither wanted to do. Several hundred dollars and their relationship seemed to be riding on this trip.

Tension produced the inevitable. Teresa complained about her seasickness once too often and Ed exploded. The argument that followed made both forget the wind and the ocean. The captain was instructed to take them back to shore. Aggravation of mutual hostility proved the victor, rather than the turbulent ocean.

Since they had paid so much money for the outing, and were not altogether comfortable being together, they felt forced to enjoy the trip. The irony, as they later related it, was that eighty cents' worth of bait brought them more enjoyment than two hundred dollars' worth of boat. When two seek to reestablish their relationship, it is easier to do it inexpensively, since expectations or demands for enjoyment will then be not as impossibly high.

Simple acts of thoughtfulness carefully placed and properly timed can turn the tide for two people who have lost touch with each other. In fact, the modest approach is less risky than all-out attempts to impress the other. Then a companion is not forced to respond when unready, and other attempts can be made without undue discouragement.

Since little stability can be assumed today about any kind of intimacy, whether it is called living together or marriage, occasional efforts to revive the old closeness are necessary. If nothing else comes to mind, think back to early courtship practices and retrace your steps. A walk through the park, supper at a diner, a trip to a drive-in movie, watching people from a street corner or a visit to a neighborhood tavern, when accompanied by the same pleasurable awkwardness felt on a first date trying to decide whether or not to hold hands, can provide laughs and stir dormant passions.

*Give up the advantages of feeling number two in your relationship.* Surprisingly, those that feel overlooked by their partners have several advantages. They can complain louder, gripe longer and blame their partners more easily than those feeling adequate and responsible for themselves. Unlike Harry Truman, they are incapable of saying "The buck stops here." Anyone assigning himself an underdog position in a union is free to give the other catcalls from his self-created peanut gallery or try to knock the other off his perch, much as children do in the game called King of the Mountain. Moreover, sympathy is given by loyal friends and family members who see how insensitively number two is being treated.

To give up this victimized position, one must be willing to accept responsibility for himself, claim for himself all needs and feelings as his own without attributing them to another, and tell his companion, "Move over, buddy, there are going to be *two* 'number ones' in this relationship." All this can be done without downgrading either partner.

Most people who feel second to their mate and desperately want a more important place stubbornly hold on to their humble position. It gives them a sense of security. Insecurity comes when one says yes to feeling more esteemed in a bond, since the unknown is feared and changing positions can create uncertainty and pain.

The more dominant partner can give a helping hand without either pulling himself or herself down to a secondary place or undermining the other's attempt to move up in terms of self-image.

To twist oneself loose from a number two position, one must learn to pursue separate interests, give up the feeling that the mate always has it better, and wholeheartedly share pleasurable experiences with the partner.

*Treat yourself as number one, and let your partner do likewise.* Within a relationship one person cannot prevent the other from feeling worthwhile and valuable, any more than he or she can force upon the other a necessary sense of self-importance. Both must recognize and feel that each is equally important to a healthy union.

When one moves far ahead of the other through achieving personal goals, the other should realize that he or she has the same opportunity for action, even though there is less desire to take it. That does not make the achieving individual better or worse than the less ambitious one. It simply means they are different. The point of contact is their quality of closeness, which has nothing to do with attainments.

There must be room in intimacy for both partners to be unique. Even though vastly different in talents, abilities, and attainments, two people in an intimate relationship are equal. When this bond of equality is cherished, there is no longer the compulsive need to either compare oneself with or downgrade the other.

*Recognize that intimacy is not competitive but cooperative.* When one or both people in a relationship are aggressively competitive outside the home, it is easy for this attitude to seep into their more private lives. Arguing over who talks the most, plays the best game of tennis, reads the most worthwhile books, stays the trimmest or spends the most money can continue forever. Its only reward is self-righteousness or smugness, and a growling partner.

Intimacy is basically a cooperative venture, and those that make it overly competitive, either directly or subtly, only succeed in distancing one another. Sometimes competition may clarify differences between two people, but mostly it brings rancor and grimness to a union.

Learning to be generous with one another allows each to win at different times and stops the overriding desire to destroy the other. Humor is a potent tranquilizer for emotions that become too heavy. It helps shift the emphasis from tension and anger to lightness and laughter, and each can loosen up without having to calculate whether one or the other is ahead, behind, above, or lower in importance.

At some point in living together both must stop and recognize they are on the *same* side. They are not natural enemies caught in an evolutionary spiral. Nor are they Roman gladiators fighting until one dies. Approaching one another cooperatively means both can find satisfaction in their friendship.

Competitive attitudes come from a wish for recognition and esteem, which, given the atmosphere of hostility, will not be fulfilled. Cooperation makes it easier to find important feelings together, since nothing is done at a mate's expense. Closeness comes naturally when it is accepted as part of cooperatively sharing life together.

# Checking Your Relationship

1. Do you practice emotional equality at home? Are there ways in which this can be further encouraged without causing undue stress in either of you?
2. Are you both able to feel special to each other? If not, has that feeling been affected by time?
3. Does your relationship usually work with ease when you are with your partner?
4. Do you find that outside interests, people and activities are disturbing your relationship? Are there ways this can be eased by finding significant time together?
5. What is important to you in intimacy with your partner?
6. Do you feel there should be a boss at home, or can you distribute responsibilities according to abilities in each partner?
7. Do you think men and women are different emotionally and intellectually? If so, how? What are the similarities between the sexes?
8. If you feel victimized by your partner at times, have you found ways to gain a more important place with yourself and your mate?
9. What can each of you do for each other that will indicate the positive way you feel? Are you aware of the actions your partner considers as signs of thoughtfulness?
10. Are career ambitions seen as a help or hindrance to either of you? Do you see them as adding or taking away from your relationship?

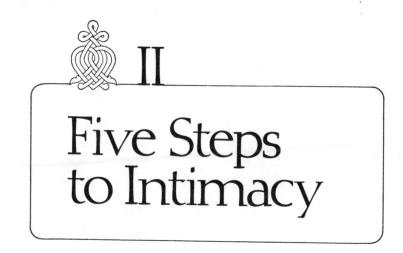

# II

# Five Steps to Intimacy

# 7

## Step One: Liking Each Other

"LIKING" A COMPANION SOUNDS INADEQUATE AS A BASIS FOR living together. Surely there must be more to it than that. Where is the sacrament and the mystery? Where are the complicated rituals that bind two together? Many people can be liked, but isn't there only one true love?

"Love" sounds majestic, romantic and lofty. Describing intimacy in mundane terms seems like an act of ingratitude to those in the past who have written so nobly of love's virtues. But it is not as iconoclastic as it seems. Even poets have found the sublime in the commonplace.

Goethe once wrote, "Love is an ideal thing, marriage is a real thing; a confusion of the real with the ideal never goes unpunished." Understanding this simple truth provides the practical basis for a life of intimacy with another.

Plainly, "liking" a companion as a basis for intimacy has been underestimated by most people. We seek solutions to intimate problems through scientific discoveries, novel approaches, new psychological theories or even from neighbors. So most people think that the emotional base for a relationship so complex must be more abstruse than something so uncomplicated as simply liking a fellow human.

## Three Reasons Why "Liking" Works for a Couple

*Liking is knowing.* Since the 1930s family sociologists have developed an impressive body of data indicating factors that influence successful mate selection. Even scientific computer dating has replaced the old storefront matchmakers of generations past. But all to no avail. Few individuals choose to use this impersonal method for picking a partner. Most still follow their primitive hunches about potential mates.

Looks and personality traits are considered in making the choice. Education, intelligence, values and socioeconomic status also influence the decision. But primarily it is still based on sexual attraction and mutual esteem. However, once the initial ardor dies down—and for most people today that happens sooner than might be expected—the folly is seen.

At that juncture, if there is liking and caring in the relationship, the couple will stay together. Though most people avow an idealistic love for all mankind, few would foolishly say they personally like everyone they meet. Yet couples come together on blind love without considering one another's temperaments and how these will determine the quality of their future together. Regrettably, some couples don't take time to know one another deeply, whether they have been together one or twenty years. For such people, a decision to end a relationship is based on an amorphous feeling that can be stated only in a general way:

"I no longer love her."

"I just can't stand being around him, but don't ask me why."

"I feel trapped and want to leave."

"We never have fun anymore, it's boring."

"He disgusts me when he wants sex."

When asked why such vague feelings exist, many cannot easily give an explanation. It takes time and understanding to discover why one has an aversion to a mate. Therefore, leaving a mate is as incomprehensible as entering the partnership. Both actions are the result of crude and ill-defined urges that impulsively lead some humans through life in a hit-or-miss fashion. Maybe we're not so far from our aboriginal ancestors, after all.

However, instincts can be educated and trusted. Just as one learns to be discriminating about foods, clothing, art, books and other artifacts of civilization, companions can differentiate attributes in one another that are pleasing or displeasing to them. This educational process requires interest, time, an open mind, cooperation and a willingness to enjoy one another. When a couple have gained a good understanding of each other, those qualities emblazoned on the banners of couples today—independence, companionship, equality and mutual support—can be discussed and applied to the union.

Despite all the glamour attached to the free life today, there is nothing more desolate for a human being than moving through life, bumping into people, mating for a fleeting moment, and then moving on without any more knowledge of another person than one had before. Many people have been jostled, pushed, shoved, nudged or even rubbed, but few have been *touched* in a manner that makes a meaningful difference. Behind the closed doors of intimacy one has an opportunity to discover the wonderful individuality of human life.

The capacity to trust one's instincts is learned. A person gradually understands the traits in himself and his companion that wear well with time. Attributes that look good from a distance may not be the same qualities that are appreciated in intimate bonds.

*Liking is flexible.* There is a carefree quality in liking a companion. It is leisurely and casual—like a dance. Partners who have danced together know when to touch, when to turn by themselves and when to move together. They create their own poetry through motion. In the same way togetherness sometimes brings a couple close and at other times allows distance as each pursues separate careers, interests or hobbies.

Liking each other means that two people value their relationship above personal differences. This flexibility indicates that a couple can embrace divergent positions on issues and still be friends. It makes no difference when a cause is championed by one and opposed by the other, whether it involves feminist concerns, political leanings, health foods, exotic and esoteric cults, physical fitness, or religious affiliation.

Caring respects the right of the other to be different. And it also knows the limits of this divergence, that is, the extent to which an issue can be taken without harming the relationship. Dissimilar attitudes do not destroy a couple who continue to like one another. Instead, these contrasting views create an enjoyable mix and produce growth for both.

Inflexibility is a greater enemy to intimacy than a partner who jeers at one's cherished ideas or schemes. Even when disagreements involve the future of a couple's relationship, liking each other allows space for both to hold contrasting views. If nothing more, a pair knows when to leave each other alone rather than forcing a disgruntled compromise.

Ironically, a couple determined to build their union with the utmost care can actually damage it and end up with the opposite of what they intended. Two people committed to "honest communication" as a principle of living together have been known to clobber each other with endless and unnecessary revelations about their psyche. Chic couples have established elaborate blueprints for living together, only to find themselves strangled by unyielding rules and strictures. Religious pairs, dedicated to rarefied ideals, have on occasion entangled themselves in pledges impossible to honor. Countless couples have scrupulously built a perfect house of cards which was bound to tumble at the slightest jar.

Inflexibility is also expressed in numerous customary and unthinking ways when the manner of relating is stubborn and unbending. A companion practices mind control by demanding identical thinking from his or her mate. One's unilateral decisions are not understood by a partner, and create conflict for both. Continual insensitive actions are not forgiven by a partner because they—and the apologies—are repeated over and over again. All these forms of rigidity become galling to couples not linked by a genuine liking for one another.

The flexibility brought by liking one another allows companions to live with normal *uncertainties* inherent in a relationship. One's love for another cannot be promised for years to come, neither can either partner feel entirely free of conflicts between togetherness and wanting to be alone. Signs of permanence, such as houses, children, and settled careers, sometimes mean that exciting adventures must be given up.

Couples who have learned to trust and like one another through repeated good experiences together can also have trust in the progress of their relationship, even though the future is unknown. Everything does not have to be decided now, tied neatly in a package this moment, problem-solved today or planned fully years in advance. Indecision and ambiguity are sometimes realistic and practical necessities in living.

*Liking deepens with time.* All couples who remain together for any length of time develop a "fit" together—that is, their expectations and needs dovetail in a manner more or less suitable to each. The best "fits" are found in pairs that still care a great deal for one another. Those who are less successful in matching their needs and expectations feel uncomfortable, irritable and unhappy together.

Misfitted couples are fussy. Personal habits in one another are criticized endlessly: one is either too messy or clean, overly talkative or quiet, or abnormally aggressive or passive. These pairs erroneously think that changing certain traits in a mate provides the necessary tailoring.

Liking one another permits a couple to mesh their needs and expectations with greater ease. In this process, pairs either develop a complementary relationship or a symmetrical one. In the first, one partner may need more security, which the other provides, while the more steady one benefits from the other's greater sense of adventure. Both adjust to differences in each other, but still champion their own particular needs. In a symmetrical relationship, such needs as security, dependence, aggressiveness, sexuality and new experience are proportional in both people.

When two people have tailored a union to fit their personalities—something not always deliberately or consciously done—touchiness about a variety of personal idiosyncrasies are less likely to arise. Common relationship imbalances expressed as feeling "overly dependent," "trapped," "distant," or "cut off" do not occur as often.

Through progressive agreeable experiences together, understanding previously unknown capacities and moods becomes more likely. No one can know another in a short period of time, though two people may meet for the first time and feel instant attraction. It takes time and a variety of circumstances, both pleasant and stressful, to discover how another human behaves. Liking one another facilitates this process.

Interestingly, when a couple arrives in a marriage counselor's office already feeling that they are mismatched, some are pleasantly surprised to learn the opposite is true.

Chris and Peter A. were such a couple. Married two years, childless, and each pleased with separate careers, they had every right to expect more happiness and less conflict together. Yet they behaved like spiteful kids. Both were determined not to allow the other any advantage in spending money, doing things with friends, taking responsibility for practical necessities or changing schedules.

But this scene did not last. When they were willing to sort out differences, discuss needs openly and rediscover the likable parts of each other's personalities, the conflicts subsided and understanding gradually replaced frustration. At this point, as with many other couples who stop arguing, an odd thing happened. They sat quietly looking at each other quizzically, not knowing what to say. Both felt as awkward and self-conscious together as two teenagers do on a first date. Several discoveries came out of this ambience of bewildering silence.

Pete spoke up first. "I respect Chris because she didn't let me walk all over her, even though I didn't like it at the time. However, it wasn't getting us anywhere. I had decided we were going to either stop the arguments or break up." Then Chris spoke about the changes in herself. She said, "I've had scales on my eyes for a long time as far as Pete was concerned. He did nothing but turn me off. I'm beginning to see him differently for the first time. I didn't think he cared, but now I know he does. What a revelation."

This was a beginning for both, a chance to care again, and it was experienced together with much the same gentleness, tenderness and concern a proud parent has for a newborn baby. At that point, they had an opportunity to build a union that better fitted the needs of both.

The way two people fit together is crucial for their happiness, and is largely dependent upon whether they like each other. If they do, chances are greater that a couple will find a bond that will continue to be comfortable to each.

## Learn to Accept What Liking Provides

Many people start living together or marry with hopes that their companion will change, or that better circumstances will enable both to be different. These kinds of assumptions prevent enjoyment of the present and actually make chances for future modification more difficult.

A couple cannot begin a union with an emotional deficit in one or the other and expect it not only to disappear but move to a plus state in one giant step. There are several steps in between, even though our rich fantasy lives tell us that dreams come true magically. Companions often make each other preposterous promises which are actually believed by both, but which never come true.

Amy and Todd H. lived together for six months. Amy was a competent, assertive businesswoman who demanded what she wanted. Todd was likewise ambitious, with plans for medical school and a career in preventive medicine. However, he was a quiet and unassertive person. When they began living together, she extracted from him a promise to speak up and commit himself on whatever came up between them, or else she would leave.

Although she liked his "little boy" quality—his nonthreatening tenderness, concern and humor—she also found his passivity offensive. He had to change. Todd, likewise, appreciated her forthrightness and competence, but found her overbearing at times. Yet he was extremely fond of her and strongly wanted to please. Their typical interaction involved her sitting in judgment on his behavior as a Marine drill instructor might do, while he nervously attempted to satisfy her wishes. As a result, both spent most of their time together in frustration; while straightening him out, they had little time to enjoy their lives together. Their relationship was headed for failure unless she could give up her need to change him, and he likewise could stop trying to alter himself for her.

The irony is that change does not occur when forced but is more likely to happen when qualities liked in one another are accepted and prized. Todd never became assertive in all the ways Amy desired, but he did learn to speak up for himself, and she learned to soften her personal crusade to reform him. However, these changes came about only when both were able to accept each other as they were—with both good and bad traits.

Intimacy between two people is always readily available, but it can't be packaged and saved for a brighter or calmer day. Either it is appreciated today, or the time never comes. It is like the biblical manna used by the Israelites on their trek through the Sinai desert, which had to be eaten daily or it became "wormy" and rotted. Many unhappy couples never realize this. Busy complaining about the past or anxiously hoping for the future, today is never savored in uncomplicated and effortless ways with a companion. Focusing on hard work or responsibilities, many people think it is hedonistic or self-indulgent to accept the joy of living together in the moment.

## How Liking Lets You Change

Liking is not pushy, forceful or demanding. It is supportive of one another's wishes to develop, change and grow.

There are many ways a relationship changes with time. To begin with, a predominant characteristic admired in a companion while dating can be troublesome later. Ambition and assertiveness, initially respected in a partner, soon leaves the other mate puffing to keep up. Impulsiveness in one that provided fun for both afterward makes a companion worry about the other's irresponsibility. Sensuality once enjoyed in the freshness of a relationship is subsequently seen as an unfair demand for affection. Calmness and serenity honored initially by a companion become boring with time. Unexpectedly the very qualities originally pleasing to a mate become questionable as a union matures.

Why is that? People and their needs change. Adjustment to these changes is both necessary in living, as well as in living together. A perfect companion is not found, since by the time one has found *the* right person, other traits not possessed by that person are desired. Flawless companions exist only in the minds of flawed mates. No one who has any sense of discrimination is absolutely satisfied with an intimate any more than he is fully pleased with himself. Furthermore, living together is often a trade-off. For example, intelligence and wit in one are traded for compassion and attractiveness in the other. All the superior qualities one admires cannot exist simultaneously in any single human being.

Folklore says opposites attract. This is not exactly true. More accurately, opposites *create* one another. Through an intimate bond two people often unknowingly develop polarities as the result of dominant characteristics in one mate being recessive in the other. Mike C. is gregarious and likes to talk. However, with his wife, Jessica, he tends to be quieter, while she, although reserved with friends, is more open with Mike. They have created their own distinctive relationship through qualities not apparent to others.

The possibilities for such polarities are endless in any couple and revolve around numerous axes: dependence-independence, passivity-aggressiveness, optimism-pessimism, affection-distance, dominance-submission, neatness-disorderliness and so on. Ordinarily couples complement one another on these differences so both can profit. Sometimes one or more needs, such as affection or independence, exist in equal proportions in both, and so their relationship is symmetrical in certain areas.

All this is to say that the natural manifestation of polarities has important implications for both choosing a mate and living together. Needs are always expressed in terms *relative* to one's partner. No one is always dependent or independent, neat or sloppy, affectionate or distant, but compared with one's partner, usually one is more one way than the other.

Problems arise through imbalances in this system. When a mate accuses the other of being overly dominant, that mate is behaving that way only because the other is submissive, and the reproach itself forces him or her to be more dominating. Change therefore happens *first* in oneself in the direction desired, and a partner is then influenced naturally to change, in order to live with a mate.

Therefore, blaming and pushing a companion are self-defeating, since they force both people into rigid and fixed polarities that do not easily change. The only person anyone can ever change in a relationship is oneself. Attempting to make the other person more affectionate, less dependent, neater or more talkative usually influences him or her to be just the opposite. Natural stubbornness and resistance make such efforts completely counterproductive and dangerous to any union.

Liking a companion eases the whole process of change. When enough is found in a partner that can be appreciated and enjoyed, a viable relationship is present, and, surprisingly, a person is more likely to change in the way both desire.

Companions *always* viewing one another in the same manner are in trouble. A person is not "always" pessimistic, lazy or selfish, and it is only a reflection of one's own lack of perception to mock a partner in this manner. Liking one another leaves room for both to change, grow and develop together.

Change is a natural part of living and of living together. However, there are a few rules that could be followed to achieve it. Sometimes they run counter to the obvious desire to force a partner to be different. Desirable changes are more likely to occur for partners who have not bullheadedly polarized their needs or insisted that the other be different. A relationship can also be changed by one partner modifying his behavior; this alteration will contribute to change in both.

Whether attempting to change an annoying habit in a partner, such as leaving soiled clothes lying around, one must show the other what is meant by changing one's own behavior. After requests are made that are unheeded, ignoring the soiled clothes is more effective than nagging. Similarly, simply showing concern for a mate who is having difficulty coping with a situation without giving in to his helplessness is more productive than overdoing for a partner in a manner that may breed resentment.

Liking one another facilitates change in both. At least there is a minimal desire to consider a companion's wishes, and do the obvious things that please. More important, it gives both a *choice* to be different without undue pressure.

## Find Companionship with Your Partner

Most couples value companionship highly, but few know how to achieve it. This is a chief complaint among couples when their relationship goes awry.

Donna and Brian H., a handsome young couple in their late twenties, felt bored with each other. Married for a year, they had previously lived together two years. Their disenchantment with each other came gradually. Early in their relationship companionship was exciting—wine and cheese, long talks. Brian bought a sailboat that slept two, so weekends could be spent on the lake. But they grew tired of being together without friends. They tried playing doubles in tennis as a couple, but it eventually led to arguments. A couples' bridge club was their next experiment, but Brian was too serious about his game, and often reduced Donna to tears through embarrassing name-calling.

If there ever was a couple that believed in togetherness, it was Brian and Donna. But it did *not* bring companionship. Pairs like this once prompted Philip Wylie, a social critic of the forties and fifties, to write a scathing essay, "To Hell with Togetherness."

Togetherness is not companionship—a myth commonly held by couples. "Doing things together" is not the answer to unhappy unions. In fact, it can engender more ferment than existed before, as it did with Donna and Brian. Pairs typically have dissimilar interests. One prefers hockey games, while another fancies the symphony or theater. Another partner likes to rebuild antique cars, while his mate enjoys macramé. Forcing one another into activities not enjoyed or appreciated is asking for trouble. This is not to say that one cannot share interests with a mate simply because one wants company; what is meant is doing things together is a non-essential for companionship.

Nor does camaraderie require participation in strange and esoteric practices that supposedly bring enlightened communication. Variety in sexual technique may be enjoyable, the mélange of Eastern mystical introspection may give impetus to living, mind-altering drugs may bring pleasure, faddish psychological jargon may give insight into human nature, but jointly indulging in all these is not necessarily companionship. Nor is it having the same intellectual interests, career ambitions or sensitivities. Companionship finds its sublime fulfillment through easily sharing the myriad moods that compose life: sadness, happiness, tension, frustration, weakness, pridefulness, depression, vulnerability, tiredness, tenderness, irritableness, toughness, joy and any other state of mind. When partners have learned to simply share these moods, they have companionship. It can be cherished a few minutes a day or broadened through hours of intense conversation. Whether discussing the mundane necessities of living or matters of consequence, it can be equally appreciated. From any angle one chooses, the truth of essential companionship is the same—it is sharing all of life together.

Companionship gives credence to all the moods of a human. They can be tolerated if not always accepted. In fact, it encourages one to be human, even when one is afraid of one's own humanity. The more a pair accepts in each other, the greater the depth and richness of their union, and the finer the expression of intimacy discovered.

Companionship is similar to any good friendship. Although a partner does not have to be a best friend, he can be a *good* friend. Sharing comes easily to those who feel kinship with one another. Liking and caring are felt naturally. Sexual satisfaction brings increased pleasure. The gratification of living together is like being with good friends.

## Checking Your Relationship

1. What are the qualities you like and prize in your partner? Do they offset his or her annoying traits, so that they seem less consequential? Telling a mate about the things you like in him or her helps both of you.
2. Is there enough room for change and growth in your relationship so that both of you can enjoy it more fully? What can you do to expand this possibility?
3. Do you both feel a basic acceptance of each other so that living together allows you more options for growth?
4. How do you define companionship and what are the necessary conditions for finding it with your partner? Can you enjoy being together at times without any planned activity?
5. Do you allow room for separate interests and pursuits without its being a threat to your relationship?
6. If you have been divorced or been through a broken love relationship, do you have some sense of why it failed? Do you know both your part and your partner's part in the failure and have you been able to profit from this understanding?
7. Do you have a general sense of the kind of relationship that works best for you?
8. Can your love feelings remain basically unaffected by specific negative qualities you find in your mate?
9. Do you find commitment follows naturally for you once you are aware of the importance of your partner to you?
10. What in your relationship would you like to see change so that it can be more enjoyable to both of you?

# 8

## Step Two: What You See Is What You Get

EVERYONE MAKES MISTAKES AT TIMES IN APPRAISING OTHER people. Voters, juries, employers, family members and friends have been deceived in judging the character of others. Even the most astute psychiatrists and psychologists have misread other humans. Is it any wonder, then, that companions at times feel they have been duped, fooled or misled by a mate?

Understanding the human mind—even one's own—is tricky. Inside a close relationship, where subjectivity is predominant, this is particularly true. When the comic Flip Wilson, dressed as his female counterpart Geraldine, seductively says, "What you see is what you get," everyone laughs. But this phrase has much more meaning for pairs than being just a funny line.

"What you see is what you get" is present when two people see each other in purely idyllic terms. But it also exists later when that same pair see each other at their most despicable and degenerate. And likewise it is there on another occasion when they see each other as a reliable and congenial companion. Can people change that much? It is doubtful that couples can alter themselves that drastically; the real changes lie in their *perceptions* of one another. In intimacy, how one is seen depends largely upon the satisfaction or pleasure one gives to a mate. A relationship can always be judged by the amount of gratification enjoyed by each.

Problems arise when one sees the other as an extension of his needs and not as a separate person, or expects a mate to live up to a romantic ideal, or sees himself or herself as the more important of the two. Inability to view oneself and one's partner sensibly always leads to discord.

In addition, there is a natural slackening of the intensity of initial love. As in any first experience entered with hope and expectation—whether starting a career, beginning a hobby, finding a friend or going on a vacation—there is disillusionment, since reality is never as perfect as one's dreams.

When a pair risks living together, they learn there is a difference between what they wish in a mate and what they receive. Learning about these differences is the strong reason couples give for living together before marriage.

Ted W., a graduate student, met Marie K. in one of his classes. She was happy, bright and friendly with almost everyone. They dated several months and then decided to live together. He felt she was a gem, and thought he was a lucky man. But Marie was different from what he expected. Though usually she was vibrant and full of life, sometimes she was moody in a way that confused Ted. Sometimes depression engulfed her and she was irritable with him. Initially he was shocked, but after talking with her and reflecting upon her unpredictable moods, he decided she was no different than he—he, too, had his ups and downs. Although he still respected her, he realized she was not the perfect companion he had imagined she would be—any more than he was.

## How to Live with Irreconcilable Differences

Periodically a news item reports that a notable personality has filed for divorce. Often the reason given is "irreconcilable differences." Whether this is a legal designation or the celebrity's polite way of telling the public that the divorce is none of its business, the terminology sounds impressive and legitimate. Certainly, no one could or should live together under those circumstances.

Whether or not they realize it, all couples live together under the same circumstances—with "irreconcilable differences"—

throughout the entire life of their union. The reason is that humans are totally unalike. This dissimilarity is a fact of life that is joltingly present when living closely with another. Conflict reminds a pair they are different, but they usually refuse to reconcile themselves to this simple fact. Rather, they tend to see one another in derogatory terms, and when taken to extremes, a companion takes on diabolical and sinister qualities.

Attempts to erase, deny or compromise these differences inherent in human beings lead to increased difficulties. Why do people have difficulty accepting their companions at face value without attempting to make them over? There are numerous reasons, but here are some of the most important:

—Differences make a partner feel separate and alone.
—The misconception of togetherness makes partners feel they must minimize differences.
—A separate autonomous being means that a mate is not available to meet all one's needs.
—Since no companion is flawless, one must face the other's inner weaknesses and not expect him or her to conceal imperfections.
—Conflict is inevitable when there are too many differences.
—Different desires in one cannot always be satisfied by the other.
—Some companions view unlikeness between themselves in judgmental terms of right and wrong and thus only one is correct—a situation difficult to tolerate.

However, acknowledging one's differences with a mate does not have to be as traumatic as some would make it. In fact, it can bring pleasure and fulfillment to both. It is possible for couples to savor and relish a union that openly recognizes unlikeness in each. Accepting dissimilarities found in one another has significant implications for living together. "Compromise," that nasty word people associate with living together, is unessential. Partners can still pursue separate careers or even separate vacations and still have companionship. People only complain about compromising when they are not flexible in dealing with one another. Living involves exchanges in many ways—that is, for anything gained something else must be given up.

Furthermore, accepting differences makes possible a wide

disparity of interests. A female physician marries a long-distance truckdriver, and both find a way to make their relationship viable. Neither gives up his or her work, but both highly value the limited time spent together.

Couples forced to separate because of military careers, employment requirements or schooling still find ways to stay intimate. The crucial factor is not compromise or similar interests but a desire to make things work. When a couple's arrangement, however complex, is more than worth it for both, they find intimacy.

Alice T., a newly appointed history professor at a Northern university, decided to leave her husband of fourteen years. She moved to another town with her twelve-year-old daughter, Pam, and her Siamese cat. Her husband, Mac, a salesman by profession, begged her to stay. When he insisted they were good friends and had great sex together, she said that this was true, but that they were intellectually incompatible. She wanted someone who shared her sensitivities to life, and frankly, someone who did not embarrass her around friends as he often did by his gauche behavior. Mac was crushed when Alice eventually divorced him.

Several years later Alice found a more compatible man, someone who also taught at the university. At first, she was extremely happy with her new man, Tom. Then doubts arose. For one thing, Tom was less interested in sex than she, and at times was impotent. Also, he demanded more exclusive time with her than Mac had, and she liked her social life with others.

All this made her doubt whether she had made the right decision in leaving Mac. Emotionally she liked Mac more than Tom, but still felt drawn to Tom because of their similar interests. Eventually she learned to face the fact that there are "irreconcilable differences" with any mate one chooses.

## Deal with Disappointments Directly to Find Intimacy

Most people do not wish to be reminded of their disappointments in life, and rightly so. There is no profit in dwelling on incidents that brought sadness. Whether it was a special vacation canceled, bad judgment that ruined career plans, a friend that didn't help in time of need or children that failed to live up to one's hopes for them, disappointment is a common human experience that only too poignantly reminds us of our vulnerability. The manner in which disappointments are handled has crucial importance for the survival of an intimate relationship.

Partners often do strange things when there is dissatisfaction in living together. Some *deny* that it exists. Parents of a beautiful two-year-old daughter, Betty and Tim K. were "happily" married for five years when Betty unexpectedly decided to leave. Why? She said, "I'm unhappy. Tim is a grouch. We used to spend time together having fun. Now all he thinks about is his job, job, job. He's forgotten me. Life is too short for that. I want to start over and find someone else."

Earlier, when she had commented on their dull relationship Tim thought her complaints were silly and would say, "Everything is going to be all right. You know I have to work." She would feel she had been reproached and would be quiet. However, the threat of divorce made Tim discover that his wife and child were much more important to him than he had realized. But it was too late. Sustained efforts by him to alter the situation were not welcomed by Betty. The denial of unhappiness had existed too long to reawaken loving feelings in her. They sadly separated and later divorced.

Other people behave differently when their hopes for a good union are thwarted by a companion. They attempt to forcibly *change* the source of disappointment, namely, their mate. Pressuring a partner is as unsuccessful as denial. In the parent-child relationship even a word of caution can backfire. Mom says to Johnny, "Don't put that pea in your nose—the one you're playing with!" After she leaves, Johnny thinks to himself, That's not a bad idea, I think I'll try it—and the pea goes into the nose. In the same way, people tend to become mulish when they think others are trying to push them. Ready to leave for a dinner party, Don W. says to his wife, Marty, "Hurry up, we're going to be late." Marty responds, "I'll be there in a minute." A minute passes and Don yells, "Dammit, I'm leaving without you." Marty screams back, "You know I can't be rushed. Go to hell if you can't wait." From such small beginnings couples proceed to pressure one another in larger ways:

"Why can't you do a better job of handling finances?"

"Start spending more time with the children, they need you."

"Why don't you listen when I'm talking?"

"You never show me love anymore."

"Can't you do anything *I* want to do once in a while?"

"I'm not going to do anything around here unless you change your attitude."

Then there are those who feel they have been deceived by the partner and *blame* him or her for misleading them, for the promises made, the behavior expected and the dreams of closeness have all failed to come true. Feeling cheated, they strike back with recriminations, which leads to further bitterness with no resolution. Couples who incessantly blame one another resemble the stormy pair in Edward Albee's play, *Who's Afraid of Virginia Woolf?* They are armed with sorrowful memories blamed on the partner.

For some, the inevitable disenchantment that occurs for all couples leads them into *self-blame*. Rather than accepting it as a phase in the relationship, they want to punish themselves. "How could I have been so stupid?" Sandra M. kept repeating to herself as she thought of failing a second time in marriage. "I felt I learned my lesson the first time, but I just repeated my mistake. I guess I'll never be happy." Brian, her husband, likewise disappointed in Sandra, supported her self-demeaning attitude by angrily agreeing with her: "You're sick. You'll never get your stuff together." With that kind of support, she needed no other enemies—including herself.

With the help and encouragement of a therapist over a period of time, Sandra decided she was not going to be defeated. When she stopped her self-flagellation, or at least limited it to fifteen minutes a day in her bedroom with sackcloth and ashes, she became a person who was more alive and available to Brian. He was shocked by the change in her and couldn't explain it away as a Machiavellian move. It forced him to alter his position with her. No longer safely a spectator in their home giving orders and catcalls from his armchair, he was obliged to join her in living or get out. Sheepishly he decided to stay, and began to treat her differently.

Others attempt to *escape* their disappointment in this difficult stage of living together. Carol R. left Tony, her husband of eight years, and two preschool boys, for Mike B. and an adventure on the West Coast. She and Mike, who was also married, had known each other for two years. The two couples socialized together and shared baby-sitters. During this time Carol and Mike grew fond of each other and thought of themselves as soulmates because they had similar views on life and wanted the same novel adventures. Carol decided that life with Tony was boring, because he had become "too serious and stuffy."

Unknown to their partners, Carol and Mike made plans to leave town together. They were seeking a new life out West. Notes left for their spouses were brief, only indicating that they were sorry their marriages hadn't worked out and that eventually a forwarding address would be sent. Carol knew that Tony could care for the boys because his family was in town and would help. In the night while Tony slept, Carol quietly kissed her two sleeping youngsters good-bye.

Three months later the soulmates were living in a rented house near Portland, Oregon. Both were working at menial jobs to make ends meet—their careers had been left far behind. Though they still loved their life together, their romance was fraying. Carol became irritable and began picking on Mike, complaining about traits previously overlooked. They argued on occasion, but nothing was resolved. She missed her two boys; the occasional telephone calls were not enough. She wanted to go home.

Carol finally returned to her children and Tony, and tried to cope realistically with the broken relationship. Both agreed a divorce was necessary. For practical reasons Carol was given custody of the youngsters and Tony visits them freely. The destructiveness to both partners and their children was at least minimized by the realistic resolution of a painful situation.

Most people are less dramatic than Carol in their attempts to escape unhappiness. Instead, they distract themselves by becoming absorbed in careers, organizations, friends, other companions, hobbies, children or even high-minded activities that serve mankind.

None of these ways of handling disappointment—denial, forcing change, blaming, self-blame or escape—is of any use. The only alternative is to accept the reality that a companion is different from what one expected.

*Recognize that disenchantment is a common transitional phase.* Knowing that almost all couples pass through this phase will put it in the proper perspective. Since this significant step toward intimacy cannot be by-passed, the sooner two people are able to take each other at face value, the greater their chances of happiness will be. Both must confront their differences, recognize their points of disharmony, and find enough enjoyment together to make the adjustments worthwhile.

*Accept without alarm the feelings that differences bring.* Differences do not always indicate that conflict is present or that a union has failed. Tolerance will eventually bring acceptance. In fact, couples that have lived together happily for years delight in one another's distinctiveness. These differences are understood and esteemed, and pose no threat to one another. Admirable qualities, such as an analytical mind, a sense of humor, a nurturing attitude, an openness to life or a capacity for managing routines, are more easily appreciated, but even negative traits—a temper, sloppiness, forgetfulness, and abruptness—can be tolerated in a comfortable bond.

## Overcome Two Obstacles to Closeness: Hurt-Collecting and Labeling

An especially virulent marital disease called "hurt-collecting" has weakened many a union from time immemorial. A case history helps illustrate the destructiveness involved. Barbara and Dick P., married eighteen years and parents of four teenagers, found their relationship debilitating because of vicious arguments that sent them off into separate corners like wounded dogs. Their fighting was never confined to immediate problems. Barbara, more afflicted with the disease than Dick, could recall every instance of pain caused by Dick in their eighteen years together. When provoked, she would dredge up a whole batch of memories to document how Dick not only mistreated her now, but had done so from the beginning. "Remember," she would say, "when I gave you money to buy yourself a wedding present from me, and instead you took it and paid for the wedding pictures? I'll never forgive you. Then you never were around when the children were born, were you? Every time I needed you, you weren't around." They stayed together for no other reason than to yell at each other. Apparently, anger was better than loneliness.

Most couples do not carry on like Barbara and Dick, but many do nurse grudges about past mistreatment. These are people who rival the IBM computer in being able to catalogue, isolate, store and retrieve information with the greatest of ease. One's inability to understand a companion's needs is taken by a mate as a certain sign of insensitivity. Thus thoughtless actions on the part of the offending partner are taken by the "hurt-collector" as deliberate assaults. As a result, both feel confused and less confident as intimates.

The other barrier to intimacy is best described as labeling. Americans love labels. From cans to cars to candidates we spend enormous amounts of time and money categorizing everything. Thanks to behavioral scientists, we have labels for all forms of behavior: neurotic, psychotic, sociopathic, etc. Some people are high achievers; others are low achievers. Mental hospitals are filled with labeled people. Schools are overflowing with tested and classified children. Hospitals and insurance companies delight in branding people. In the mental health field, when other designations do not accurately describe an individual's ills, he is labeled simply an "inadequate personality." It is the ultimate insult to a human being, and a reflection of the classifier's bias.

Labels are intended to be a shorthand method of identification and as such are necessary. But when categories are used for people, they can be a powerful support for bigotry. One only has to remember Hitler's Germany to recognize how labels were used to destroy human life.

Used inside the family, labeling has a long-lasting, detrimental effect. Children have been forced to either live *up to* or live *down* labels. Whether classified by parents as incorrigible, useless, selfish or angelic, hyperactive, unruly, or as a perfect child, a black sheep, Mama's boy or Daddy's girl, labels stick and often create immense suffering for both parent and child.

Similarly, labeling has a disastrous effect on intimacy. When one catches himself saying to a partner, "You always . . ." or "You never . . ." then one is being guilty of labeling, even when the remark is meant to be a compliment. Kind people have a right to be nasty at times. Smart individuals can be stupid. Responsible spouses can be childish. When external classifications are removed, the possibilities for change and growth increase.

False notions about maleness and femaleness also contribute to this labeling. Stereotypes learned from one's background are brought to a relationship and obstruct closeness. Men can cry. Women can think. Both sexes can be passionate. Either can worry. Traditional imprinting need not hinder a pair from exploring the corners and crevices of each other's personality. To peg a partner as *always* strong, weak, responsible, irresponsible, happy, sad, thoughtful or careless does an injustice to him or her. Although labeling may be easier than living with ambiguity, in the long run it forces each into a box and kills all hope for affirmative change in a union.

Joyce and Warren O. learned this lesson the hard way. Married six years and parents of Tina, a delightful two-year-old, they were childhood sweethearts. Joyce finished professional school early in their marriage and was now a registered nurse. Warren stayed with the same company he worked for in high school and had become a supervisor in one of its warehouses. They grew up together in the same neighborhood of a small Midwestern town.

They thought they knew each other well, but in the last several years they developed opinions about each other that threatened to snuff out their enjoyment of being together. Joyce saw Warren as "belligerent and insensitive." Warren said that Joyce had changed and was now an "insecure crybaby." She fussed at him when he made changes in their plans, and accused him of imaginary misdeeds. Both had given each other labels that became self-fulfilling prophecies. For Joyce and Warren to survive the onslaught of their labeling, they had to move beyond it by trying to understand each other better.

New shifts in their relationship came about almost as unknowingly as did their labeling. Joyce saw Warren playing with Tina on the floor one evening and realized he was still capable of tenderness; maybe he could be this way with her once in a while. The process of recognition was more difficult for Warren, until he suddenly understood the full extent of Joyce's competence: she paid the bills, cleaned the house, took care of Tina, and at the same time held a full-time job at the local hospital. She was not as helpless as he had thought. And so the labels were finally removed.

Hurt-collecting and labeling can arise when two people are unwilling to accept differences and expand their relationship. The bitter results of unsuccessful attempts to make a partner something he or she is not, these two obstacles change a union into an unholy war that both lose.

## *Learn to Take Each Other at Face Value*

By now it is obvious that the easiest and emotionally least brutal way to live together is to take one's companion at face value. It is also the only way one finds intimacy with a companion. "What you see *is* what you get," even when that reality is not completely pleasant.

Rose Franzblau, the psychologist and columnist, once described the first recognition by little boys and girls of physical differences between the sexes as "the sight that civilizes." These anatomical differences are first viewed with curiosity and subsequently with admiration.

Likewise for couples civilization intrudes at a certain point in their lives. Discovery of differences in attitudes, outlooks and aspirations between partners takes them from romantic fairyland to enlightenment with all its complexities. This is the end of innocence when they are faced with the truth of their differences.

# Checking Your Relationship

1. What are your customary ways of dealing with personality differences between you? Are they effective? How can they be made more satisfying to both of you?
2. Do you nurse grudges, or can you deal with your differences immediately and then forget them?
3. Does it make you feel more comfortable to see your partner as always being the same? Can you allow some room for change and growth?
4. How do you see yourself as being different from your partner?
5. What characteristics do you admire most in your partner?
6. Can you let each other keep his or her idiosyncrasies and still enjoy being together?
7. Can both you and your partner affirm your individuality without great threat to your love feelings?
8. Can you take each other at face value and enjoy the present together?
9. How do you feel your differences complement one another?
10. Can you at times feel strong together, and at other times feel weak as a couple? What can each do to allow *all* the moods of living to be shared together?

# 9

## Step Three: Learning to Communicate

PROBLEMS CAN ARISE INSIDIOUSLY WITHIN ANY UNION OF two people. Many couples are not aware of their seriousness until they've gotten out of hand: financial debt forces drastic action; an extramarital affair is discovered; children develop unmanageable problems; communication breaks down; sex loses its appeal; love is gone; separation seems inevitable. Shocked senseless, a couple wonders, "How the hell did we get in this mess?"

Can such disasters be prevented? They can, when partners learn to communicate in the midst of the inevitable conflict that living together brings. They must first realize that because of the disparity in individual preferences, the possibilities for disagreements by partners are legion.

If you will, step inside Pat and Bruce G.'s bedroom with me. This may seem voyeuristic, but we'll stay only long enough to get a glimpse of the conflict that upset their relationship in a few weeks' time. As with any other couple, the bedroom of Bruce and Pat's home was the immense source of intimate pleasure, as well as the luxuriant wellspring of enough conflict to keep them busy the rest of their lives.

The scenario begins one quiet evening as they are getting ready for bed.

"I saw the perfect water bed for us today down at Winkles," Bruce says. "Let's buy it!"

"No, I can't stand those things. I tried Ginny's out a few days ago and it made me seasick. Let's keep our double bed or get a king-size."

. . .

"Why do you insist on closing that damn window? You know it's healthier to get fresh air while you're sleeping," Bruce says.

"I get cold, and, besides, I'm tired of all that health stuff you keep throwing at me."

. . .

"Come on to bed, honey, it's late," Bruce yells to Pat while she's still in the den. Walking swiftly toward the bedroom, Pat says gruffly, "When are you going to learn I'm a night person and don't like to go to bed with the chickens?"

"Well, you sleep more than I do, anyway. You never get up first and fix breakfast. I read somewhere that the first up in the morning is the servant, and the other is the master. Don't you feel bad about me fixing breakfast?"

"Why should I. You know I've got my own work to do. Don't you understand that?"

. . .

Snuggled together in bed with Bruce, Pat thinks out loud, "Let's have another child. I think it's a mistake for Jennifer not to have a brother or sister."

"Now, we've been over that ten thousand times. We can't afford it on my salary—not until I'm more settled in my work."

Pat says in a tight voice, "That might be five years from now."

. . .

After a few amorous exchanges in bed Pat whispers, "Make love to me." Jerking away from her, Bruce says, "I'm really tired tonight, and I've got to get going early in the morning. Can't we wait till tomorrow night?"

. . .

Bruce cuddles up to Pat and both relax. He holds her a moment and she says, "Would you mind staying on your side of the bed tonight? I'm in no mood. It's been an awful day."

Bruce jumps out of bed and says, "If that's the way you feel, I'll sleep on the sofa." He grabs a blanket and storms out of the room. Pat is wide awake and won't go to sleep for a long time. Neither will Bruce.

Bedrooms have weighty meanings for couples. Passions are expressed. Angers are voiced. Not only goals, hopes and dreams but differences are discussed. And intimacies are shared. The setting is the rich source of all the jointly held and private rumblings of both partners while awake and asleep. Here conflict between two people is inescapable.

## Six Principles of Effective Communication

Troubled couples attempting to communicate through complex and circuitous means feel as frustrated as harried parents trying to decipher the maze of directions that come with unassembled toys. But communication need not be so difficult. Here are some guidelines that make it simple, direct and forthright.

*Develop a sense of timing.* There is a rhythm to living together as real as the ocean tides. As with other tasks that require coordination, it can be learned.

In communication there is a time to talk, a time to listen and a time to leave one another alone. Success or failure in sharing thoughts in a satisfying way is largely based on knowing these times. Some people have trouble finding the rhythm of living together. They often miss the beat because they are nervous, upset, angry or self-absorbed. Requests for sex are poorly timed when previous glances and touches had only provoked irritation. Trying to argue an issue is fruitless when a companion is exhausted from a day's work. Demands to discuss family budgeting are useless when a husband has just lost a sizable contract in business. Urging responsible action is counterproductive when a mate is depressed by personal setbacks.

Trial and error, interest and concern and "laying back" at

times help a couple get in step with each other. Moving outside one's own needs long enough to discover what makes a companion tick also aids this process. Listening, expressing feelings and developing an increased awareness are invaluable.

There is a more oppressive loneliness than the loneliness of being alone. And that is being lonely while living with another. When the points of contact are purely superficial, there can be no comforting feeling that one shares life with another person, much less a mate. If two people are going to bother to live together at all, they should take the trouble to discover each other.

*Consider the climate.* Communication does not take place in an emotional vacuum. When partners are unaware of this basic fact, interaction is not possible. Different situations in a couple's life will have an ambience that can either discourage or encourage real communication. Antennae make one aware of what this ambience is.

The climate of a pair's emotional environment can be rated on a scale of one to five as follows: cold, cool, neutral, warm and hot.

When it is cool, a wayward glance by one is taken as rejection by the other. When it is neutral, physical fatigue puts one to sleep while the other is telling a touching personal story. If it is warm and a partner's passion wants to make it hot, then one must encourage his or her partner to put aside the engrossing mystery novel long enough to get in the mood. Cold climates of course, are, the most difficult, and lead to more arguments, misunderstandings and unhappiness than any of the others. In such situations a neutral or even warm atmosphere must be created before initiating any serious discussion.

Couples that suffer from tunnel vision have difficulty with effective communication. They rush at a partner with their needs, never using peripheral vision to assess the climate.

Needless to say, intimacy flourishes best in a warm climate. One may have all the latest information available, giving couples specific and complete instructions on how to talk together, and still fail miserably if the atmosphere is wrong. In the same way, a partner armed with important skills for discussing problems with children will still strike out when the environment is not considered.

Therefore it is often necessary for one or both companions to create a mood that is lighter, more relaxed or more encouraging in order to make serious talk possible. Rarely are partners able to discuss complicated problems effectively when they have fun together only infrequently. The same principle is true in conversations between parents and children. Couples that experience their relationship as grim must first find ways to enjoy it before moving into lengthy discussions that simply increase the gloominess. *When* to talk to a mate is therefore as important as *how* to talk together.

*Learn to listen all over.* Listening—that is, when one listens with body, mind and spirit—is a strenuous activity. Theodor Reik described it as "listening with the third ear." A behavioral scientist recently counted all the bits of information, both verbal and nonverbal, passed between two people in one minute and discovered they added up to an astronomical figure. Active listening consumes energy but is less exhausting than failures in understanding.

Couples frequently complain they can't communicate when first coming to a marriage counselor's office. The problem is that listening is selective for couples. Amicable messages are easier to hear than discontented muttering. Complaining is less palatable than playful banter. To make effective communication possible, *all* messages must be considered important.

Sometimes it is enough to listen, intensely, to a mate, to every nuance of his thoughts, feelings, desires and body language. Anyone who has ever been listened to in this way knows how cathartic it is. The mere act of such listening is an *end* in itself and is infinitely superior to advice or helpful action.

But listening is a two-way street. A sympathetic companion cannot listen interminably, as if he or she were a therapist. Both mates have needs and feelings; there must be reciprocity.

*Express yourself clearly.* Good communication is learned through trial and error and a continued interest in mutual awareness. Companions are able to say what they mean and mean what they say. One is able to convey the essence of who he is to a mate at any given point in time. Through words, actions, appearances, and physical contact, the message is understood by a partner. Talking is only part of it. The whole self speaks and conveys substance.

Many people have a mistaken notion of what they call productive communication. It is not talking nonstop to a mate while gulping air to prevent drowning in one's words. Nor is it telling a partner every thought and feeling one has, whether noteworthy or meaningless, in an enormous dumping action. Neither is it screaming "I'm not angry," when one is obviously furious. It is not even saying "We need to sit down and talk," and then feeling speechless and frustrated by having to make discussion into a ritual. All these forms of communication have been known to overwhelm, anger, befuddle or constrict a partner.

Direct and simple communication comes spontaneously in any circumstance when the timing is right. Wordy or wordless, sublime or silly, it is the product of knowing one another and tuning in on similar wave lengths. It is also the result of expressing oneself clearly to a mate over a long period of time.

*Recognize vulnerabilities when conflict arises.* Conflicts that come with intimate living follow a natural course. Time is needed to resolve them, as in any other personal crises. In the process strong emotions are stirred, conflicting alternatives are fought over, and consequences of decisions are considered. If dissent is freely voiced, despairing is not excessive, or fears are not magnified beyond reason, the dynamic tension of conflict can allow both to grow as persons.

In this heightened interaction, companions often become aware of specific emotional vulnerabilities in one another. For some the deficiency or flaw is related to physical appearance. For others, these Achilles' heels or weaknesses are based on emotional traumas suffered in the past, which now cause feelings of sexual inadequacy, fear of competition, feelings of not belonging or of insecurity. Arguments can open these sores, and unless couples are aware that they exist, they will be the source of unending conflict.

Bob H. grew up in a broken home. His mother deserted the family in childhood and he, along with four other siblings, was raised by his father. Since he was the oldest, the burden of caring for the family's daily needs fell on his shoulders. He cooked, cleaned and kept his brothers and sisters in laundered clothes. He saw to it they did their homework, and sent them off to school each morning. Dad worked hard and long, but because he was an unskilled worker, money was scarce. Survival was a major issue for them at all times.

After Bob finished high school, and while still at home with the other children, he was hired at an automobile manufacturing plant, where he did very well. He received promotions, made a good salary and was even able to save money. Not long after he started work, he met Martha through a friend. They dated and fell in love. She was a nurturing person and was fond of him from the beginning. They married, moved to their own home and almost immediately started a family. Both were happy and settled into enjoying a good life together.

The trouble began when they started arguing about money. Bob was miserly, while Martha enjoyed spending what they made. The quarreling grew more and more intense, and Martha threatened to leave. She felt that since both were working and had a comfortable savings account, nothing except his stubbornness prevented their spending money to enjoy life. Bob panicked at the thought of her leaving. She couldn't go, but at the same time he couldn't relinquish the purse strings—he remembered his impoverished childhood all too vividly. He became more argumentative with her and yelled at the children. In his mind he was certain that, as in childhood, the wolf was at the door. The fears and pain of his youth returned in full force. He became almost incapacitated by his anxiety.

Martha now knew that his reactions overstepped the bounds of normal worries and that professional help was needed. With the therapist's help Bob was able to face the searing hurt of his early life in a more rational way. Eventually the past stopped giving him double vision—Martha was not the wild spendthrift he made her out to be. He saw that he was still fighting battles for survival he had already won, and that now he could relax a bit and *live*. Options not possible in childhood were now available. Finally he was able to be more open with Martha. It was a poignant moment when he told her how he kept for emergencies a pillowcaseful of coins in the rafters of their recently purchased home. He had been embarrassed to tell her about it before.

It was fortunate that both had sense enough to do something about a major conflict before it destroyed them. As a result, their relationship was salvaged, and both felt closer together than ever before.

*Keep the focus specific.* At the beginning of the Paris peace talks that ended the United States' involvement in the Vietnam war, considerable time was spent deciding on the shape of the bargaining table and the placement of chairs. Some commentators felt it was ridiculous to waste precious time on such trivial matters when lives were being lost daily. But it did not turn out that way. This initial jockeying for position made it possible for both sides to size each other up and make communication easier by beginning with inconsequential matters.

The lesson for couples is twofold, especially when conflict threatens to become a devastating war. First, it is easier to argue about picayune issues like who left the soap in the sink, who didn't wash out the crockpot, or who used all the gas in the car and didn't fill it up. A whole system of interaction can be learned that teach them how to fight fairly about specific issues.

Within such a supportive atmosphere both can vent anger, voice disagreement, argue both logically and emotionally, learn how to confront each other without feeling threatened, and discover ways as a couple to resolve differences. If table-and-chairs arguments occur early in a relationship, the *first* argument does not have to be about whether or not to divorce. Those that pride themselves on peaceful togetherness are shocked when emotionally laden conflicts arise and they are unprepared to handle them. The results are usually tragic.

Second, couples that effectively communicate through their conflicts learn to keep the focus specific. In other words, if a pair is talking tables and chairs, they do not bring up a whole string of other grievances or give ultimatums that decide the fate of a union.

Maxine R. was saving a jar of homemade jam for her bridge

club. Al, her husband of twenty-three years, was looking for something to eat one evening and, rummaging through the kitchen cabinets, found the well-hidden jam. He enjoyed his snack while Maxine was out with friends. When she returned and saw the opened jar of jam, she blew her stack. "You son-of-a-bitch, you knew I was saving that jam for my bridge club."

Surprised, Al said, "I knew nothing about it, and stop yelling at me."

"I'll yell at you if I feel like it, you slob." (At this point anyone can tell they're not going to stick with the jam.)

"Since when is your bridge club more important than me?"

"Since now, you louse." (They're already one step from the original issue and going strong.)

"You don't mind taking money out of my pocket whenever you need it."

"If you gave me enough money I wouldn't have to do it. You treat me like a servant, you bastard." (Now they've gone two more steps past the first point of disagreement.)

They continued the argument into the night with both saying they were going to a lawyer in the morning. Which they did, and decided to separate.

It all started over a jar of homemade jam and ended in divorce. Somewhere early in their marriage, when it was still warm and exciting, they had failed to handle their disagreements effectively, so that the build-up of misunderstanding and anger was bound to end in disaster.

## Learn to Handle Your Fears and Angers

Fear inhibits self-disclosure while anger distorts messages directed at a companion. Although both emotions exist in varying degrees in much of human communication, when excessive they overload a couple's interaction beyond their ability to cope with it.

Some partners avoid all expression of either feeling—which is just as damaging, because emotions are part of interchanges that lubricate the lines of communication. When fear and anger are openly expressed, likes and dislikes can be understood more easily; priorities can be sorted; and differences can be clarified. Otherwise, a relationship becomes dull and barren. All humans have trouble handling both fear and anger. Afraid of saying too much, one keeps quiet. Angry, but not wishing to hurt a companion's feelings, one fumes inside. Fear of rejection keeps one from disagreeing with one's partner. Apprehensive of a domineering partner's temper, one evades confrontation. Fear makes people imagine more pain than an actual encounter will bring. Some panic at the thought of losing a mate. Others fear losing control through unbridled anger or uncontrollable crying. Fears of all sizes, shapes and forms incapacitate partners and paralyze communication.

Barbara S. harbored intense secret fears of losing Howard. Instead of telling him her worries, she pleaded with him to come home earlier on his late evenings out. When he refused, her pleas turned into bitter recriminations.

Howard cared for Barbara and was not really a poor husband. The only problem was that he didn't want a confining relationship, and on occasion enjoyed playing poker or going to ball games with male friends. He encouraged her to do the same with her friends and offered to stay with their children while she did. She refused, and his efforts to placate her by being with her at times were not sufficient. What she wanted was uninterrupted assurance of his love.

Howard was brought up in a home where family loyalty was taken for granted, while Barbara came from a family broken by divorce. It was obvious that the source of her fears and insecurities came from her unstable background. Howard, who had no fears of disharmony in family life, simply assumed they would be together forever and couldn't understand her nagging.

Not until Barbara openly admitted her deepest fears to herself and Howard were they able to view their relationship more realistically. What emerged was that it was she who was more likely to leave than he, since his apparent indifference might force her to do so. Shocked by this recognition, Howard was forced to examine his assumptions about automatic family loyalty. The understanding of Barbara's irrational fear led both to a more comfortable place with each other. A refocusing of their energies helped both to face their anxieties more directly. Both learned to express feelings, hopes and concerns with each other, and the future became more predictable.

## Seek Understanding: Not Problem-Solving

Many people view conversations with their mates primarily as hard work, because in such talks the emphasis is on resolving difficulties of one kind or another. If the only reason couples can find for living together is settling disagreements, solving problems or resolving conflicts, then there is little motivation for continuing communication or, for that matter, even their bonds.

Certainly, there are practical necessities to be considered in a relationship—responsibilities to be carried out and information to be exchanged—but the primary purpose of two people coming together is enjoyment of the relationship. When this fact is not recognized, any difficulties that arise become more troublesome. Within the context of a good relationship decision-making is a joint, rational process, with neither one exerting pressure on the other.

Compromise is necessary in problem-solving but unnecessary in understanding. Closeness enables both to understand that their good feelings together make their attempts to settle differences more than worthwhile. Such efforts then become not a chore or a duty but a necessary and natural part of living. Obstacles are removed, so that the business of living together can be appreciated.

If a pair's relationship has deteriorated through bitching and quarreling, then the initial step for improving it is to table problems for a while. This will enable the couple to share pleasurable experiences which will provide the basis for better understanding of each other. Often, simply sharing feelings, interests, concerns or disappointments is enough. Trying to force heavy-handed discussions about difficulties when a relationship is already strained only makes it more hopeless.

When understanding each other is more important than joint

problem-solving, a companion can make decisions by himself or herself, even though a partner may not be in complete agreement. Respecting differing opinions and preferences makes this possible. Partners do not have to agree on child-rearing practices, habits of spending money or vacation plans as long as they consider each other's views and do not move beyond the limits each can tolerate.

Daily living habits do not have to be similar when understanding exists between two people. Questions about mealtimes, qualities of neatness, recreational interests or responsibilities to children can be quickly resolved when both wish to please each other and at the same time satisfy their own desires.

Understanding is both a rational and emotional process. It comes from a caring effort to fathom the emotions and needs that motivate one's partner.

## Let Both Win

Competition occurs naturally between intimates as both jockey for position inside and outside their relationship. However, when competition dominates a union, communication is impossible and as a result both suffer.

George Y. was a Horatio Alger legend come true. The only son of tenant-farmer parents, he rose to prestige and fortune as a bank president. His Southern hometown political machine was grooming him for state government and then Washington.

During his ascent to power this arrogant and striving man met Carol, a sweet Southern lady. She was awed by his achievements; he recognized immediately that her gentility complemented his uncouthness. After a short courtship they married. But his competitive spirit that had carried him far in business and politics had a disastrous effect on family life. George could outargue Carol, force his way with her and generally keep her subservient. Years of such treatment made Carol fall into a deep depression. George thought she was stupid and had no sympathy for her constant crying. Other women entered his life.

Through professional help Carol emerged from her depression and began to fight back. Her scorn for him was great because he had robbed her of self-respect. George tried to maintain his dominance, but he underestimated her strength; she held her own in the ensuing battles. Divorce was inevitable, and the five children were forced to choose between parents in court.

The psychological costs of intense competition, especially when it is one-sided, are enormous. The lesson that some never learn is that an intimate union is not like a horse race—it must have two winners.

# Checking Your Relationship

1. Can you communicate your angers and fears to your partner without duress? How can this process be improved by both of you?
2. Do you consider the climate of your relationship before broaching a subject that may provoke anger or pain?
3. When communication is strained, can you call time-out and first do some things together that are enjoyable?
4. If problem-solving usually does not come easy for you two, something is missing in understanding. How can you improve your communication so that understanding is a more valid part of it?
5. What are the issues most important to you in communicating with your partner?
6. Do you find communication easier the longer you know each other, or does it become more complex? How can it be improved?
7. What are the most difficult issues for you and your partner to discuss? Can you first discuss why these issues are difficult before you talk about them?
8. Do you have a good sense of timing in communication? What would help you both know more about the best time to discuss things?
9. Are there specific vulnerabilities that either of you have which prevent effective communication? How can you acknowledge these vulnerabilities without adversely affecting your everyday living?
10. What are some of the positive ways you communicate with each other that mean the most to you?

# 10

# Step Four: What's Fair?

WHEN CONFUSION ABOUNDS FOR A COUPLE, ASKING THE simple question "What's fair?" suggests options never considered previously. Most associates assume that their love automatically teaches them fairness but unfortunately, it does not. Even love can be skewed in the direction of one's self-interest. In fact, if marriage or any other living-together arrangement were a combination of management and labor union, many partners would strike continuously. Unfair labor practices would be charged, and such grievances as emotional blackmail, fraud, malfeasance, bribery, perjury and vindictiveness would all be presented.

When companions disagree, they find it difficult to be objective. Rather than trying to sway the emotions, an appeal to each other's sense of fairness is more likely to lead to a resolution of the argument. As long as a companion doesn't believe that all is fair in love and war or, alternatively, that perfect justice should be meted out to a mate, a general basis for even-handed exchanges can be found.

Numerous couples never recognize that their union is governed by rules they often unknowingly establish together. Sharing household tasks, deciding financial arrangements, determining child-rearing practices and agreeing on sexual habits are part of a system of giving and receiving.

Two people can live a lifetime together with only a fleeting awareness that a systematic quid pro quo exists in all their interactions, whether on the level of responsibilities, expectations or needs. But couples who are aware that something is always given or received for something else, whether or not it is satisfactory, understand that fairness can be negotiated and are less likely to fall blindly into emotional traps.

A love relationship always begins with two distinct sets of assumptions held by the two companions. Terence Rattigan, the English playwright, sensitively portrayed these assumptions in his play *Separate Tables*. True coupling occurs as each gives up his "separate table" and joins the other.

This tacit mutual agreement for living together, gradually forged over a period of time as each partner gives up his or her separate assumptions, is also altered throughout a couple's lifetime as needs in each partner shift and as changes in society affect intimate living. For example, women's greater interest in a career, the socially approved tendency to have fewer children, increased divorce and remarriage rates and alternative life styles have all forced couples to reconsider their basic assumptions about living together. Partners can no longer assume that tradition, religious ceremony or legal documents will bind them together forever. Nor that a commitment which is a product of blind faith in one another will be long-lived. Today what is essential is an agreement that not only allows for change but is practical and fair.

## *Six Ground Rules for Living Together That Work*

Rules provide the boundaries to protect intimate living. Without them, couples are unnecessarily vulnerable to both internal and external pulls or pushes. No one lives without constraints, whether self-imposed or levied by society. So it is only reasonable that two people should live together with guidelines that are fair to both. The following ground rules suggest the basis for a viable way of life for a couple.

1. *Develop a comfortable contract.* Satisfactory commitment only comes after two people understand the fine print or implications of their informal contract and find it acceptable.

Living together before marriage may aid this process, but for some people it does not help any more than marriage ensures understanding an agreement. For that matter, some mates remain blind to their obligations to a mate until a crisis occurs.

Granting these limitations, a couple can still develop a verbal agreement that is comfortable for both. It is important to understand the essence of a partner's voiced expectations and to act in good faith toward each other in terms of the future.

A workable contract for a pair is relatively simple and manageable. There are four elements in this verbal agreement.

*Power must be distributed.* As with any political system, power can corrupt and absolute power can corrupt absolutely when held by only one partner; distribution of power offers a system of checks and balances. One companion cannot be trusted with complete dominance, even though he or she has the best interests of each at heart. Both partners must divide power in the various areas of living together if for nothing more than to indicate their involvement with each other.

*Financial resources must be shared.* Money is a potent symbol of power and love in an intimate union. In the past the breadwinner had an advantage in this regard, but today, sharing resources can be more clear-cut because often both partners have jobs. However, it is still a problem when finances are not pooled into one account. Apart from inheritances or resources from previous marriages, a joint banking account tests a pair's credibility with each other.

Couples can have separate funds for their personal needs, but a joint account indicates good faith in sharing collective expenses. Some workingwomen consider their funds as supplemental income—a mistake for both partners because such an attitude often breeds the resentful feeling expressed by one husband, "She can do what she wishes with her money, but my money is supposed to be 'ours.'"

Women who are full-time housewives and mothers can take consolation in the fact that their total managerial skills would cost at least $25,000 in the marketplace. This fact should make both companions aware that executive management does not come cheap, and that therefore resources must be shared.

*Decision-making is the responsibility of both partners.* Making decisions about living arrangements, vacation plans, automobile purchases, the children's education, retirement goals and necessary cutbacks in expenses are tasks to be undertaken jointly. Assumptions about segregated male and female prerogatives in decision-making must be cast aside so that each is open to the other's opinions.

When two people begin a relationship respecting each other's desires and priorities, this task is easier. The good judgment of both can be appreciated when they learn it is to their mutual benefit when each is satisfied by decisions affecting their joint living. Regrets and recriminations are less likely to occur when both enter enthusiastically into decision-making and strongly voice their opinions.

*Tasks should be assigned on a rational basis.* As both companions develop skills or abilities in various areas of living, tasks can be assigned to each other on the basis of expertise, and not through male or female stereotyping. However, because one partner has an exaggerated sense of his own competence, it does not mean he or she has the knowledge and talent to do everything. Obviously, an expert money manager is not equally proficient in child care. A competent planner is not necessarily adept at implementation. Tasks in living together are best shared in reasonable ways.

A contract that is comfortable for both contains at least these four elements and can be renegotiated as changes become necessary. Inflexibility, stubbornness, deceitfulness and emotional coercion are the only obstacles that prevent a reasonable agreement from working. Fairness to both partners is the principle that keeps it viable and ensures that it will wear well.

When a couple fails to recognize their informal agreement, the practical realities of living together more easily become issues of the heart, that is, they are viewed either as indicators of love or as the lack of it. Apart from one's fondness for a companion, carrying out these responsibilities indicate that a structure exists for both, whether or not their feelings are positive or negative at a specific time.

2. *Build trust and respect.* Most partners assume that they deserve trust and respect simply because they are partners. But realistically, it doesn't work that way. Both trust and

respect must be earned through overall behavior over a period of time.

Some couples foster mistrust through deception or unfulfilled promises, even those made in good faith. When a husband detained at work always promises to come home by a certain hour but never returns on time, his wife will feel deceived and angry. All he really has to do is to stop promising a specific time and simply call to say he'll be late.

Promising gets more companions into trouble than the alleged dastardly deed itself. Pledges to a companion to lose weight, to give up smoking, drinking or marijuana, to stop annoying personal habits, to be less argumentative or misleading, to be more loving, thoughtful or considerate, to be on time more frequently or to be less demanding sexually only serve to disappoint when they are not kept.

Integrity, a word almost forgotten in human relations, is important to partners, even when what is said is not pleasant to hear. More partners have spent an inordinate amount of energy attempting to live up to a promise, or to live down a pledge not kept, rather than simply being forthright at the outset—which would have saved all the trouble and frustration.

When trust is broken or respect is weakened, it can be rebuilt through action indicating that one has become more responsible.

3. *Remember the nonnegotiables.* In any contract or agreement a pair often assumes that loving and compassionate feelings go with the bargain. Unfortunately, they don't. It is unrealistic to expect them to do so. As with anything truly valuable in life, these feelings must be given *freely.*

Can't one beg or force a mate to show love? The answer is an unequivocal no. The situation requires a different approach, one that is positive. Caring behavior in one can cue the same in another, unless he or she is totally preoccupied with some problem or other, or is completely self-absorbed. Both can thus build up a repertoire of enjoyed responses that are shared easily. The times of discontent are easily weathered because they are interspersed between periods of concern and caring.

All the repetitious, tired phrases people use to elicit desired responses from a partner are futile:

"If you loved me you would . . ."

"Why don't you tell me you love me . . ."

"All I want from you is consideration . . ."

"You're never around when I need you . . ."

"All you think about is yourself . . ."

Most of such remarks are made in anger, frustration, anxiety or grief—hardly the state of mind to trigger a positive reaction.

If one wants compassion, show it *first.* Then a partner will more likely get the idea. This does not mean that one cannot also say how he or she wishes to be treated—only that this approach gives a mate a choice to respond in a freer way.

Kindness is nonnegotiable. Deciding whether or not to have guests for the weekend is negotiable. Thoughtfulness and concern are nonnegotiable. Deciding whether to live in a house or apartment is negotiable. All the human emotions that make one feel secure, loved or accepted cannot be bartered. They must be given freely.

When a union is gloomy, worrisome, sour or generally unhappy, one partner often expects the other to set things right, much as one would expect repair of a leaky faucet or a broken vacuum cleaner. Afraid of rejection or stubbornly insisting it is a mate's fault that life together has gone awry, partners often resist taking the first positive step toward reconciliation. Thus such couples frequently sound like two overly polite acquaintances walking together through a narrow archway and insisting:

"You go first."

"No, that's all right, you go first."

"No, I really would prefer your going first."

"You don't mind if I go first?"

"No, I would like you to go ahead."

"It doesn't bother you at all?"

"No, I *want* you to go first."

"Oh, that's nice of you . . . but . . . but you go first."

Except that companions are not so polite when they are trying to find a way out of their dilemma. They self-righteously demand that it is the other's duty to make up, or they hide their hurt behind a huffy façade and wait for conciliatory overtures. More marriages have been broken for this simple reason than many care to admit—waiting for a partner to go first either through an apology or a show of affection.

4. *Learn to bargain.* Some people are good hagglers. Others are only moderately skilled or do not care to dicker at all. However, haggling is a necessary part of any agreement between two people living together. Without negotiation a pair risks repressing desires, misunderstanding each other's intentions or crowding each other's living space.

What is bargained? Responsibilities in living together, conflicts between separate and joint interests, acceptable behavior on the part of both and, most important changes in circumstances. Changes in career interests, life styles, living with and then without children, as well as changes in external circumstances, make it imperative to renegotiate periodically.

Establishing negotiation at the outset as a principle of living together allows both to surface their sources of discontent with less of a feeling of being personally threatened. It also enables each to be more objective about his or her desires for change and to be more calm in the bargaining process because it will generally occur when both are in an amicable mood.

When a couple have identified the area of concern, half the battle is over. Many pairs mistakenly argue emotional needs at the same time they are discussing an issue that bothers them. In such a situation the emotional unhappiness must be addressed first.

Judy and Sam S. were married sixteen years and had three children. Both came from families where love was scarce, and felt a strong need for each other to fill an emotional void Though they loved each other, one problem kept rearing its ugly head—money. Sam saw Judy as a spendthrift who impulsively bought everything she saw, and wanted her to give up the charge cards before bankruptcy engulfed them. Judy, on the other hand, was certain Sam had never let go of anything in his life. He was a tough-minded businessman who knew that money should be saved. As he looked at the bills he said to himself, Why can't she be sensible about money? Angrily he would call for a family conference to discuss the budget. "Let's have a rational talk about this," he would say with clenched teeth. Judy would acquiesce meekly and agree to work on a budget again.

Judy had other troubles besides the money problem. She would say to herself, Why can't he show any affection to me or the children? I raise the kids, cook the meals, wash the clothes. I try to please him. He never does anything for me except bitch about money. She would brood for days. In the evenings Sam would hardly speak—a grunt here, a grunt there, sometimes a monosyllabic word.

Some mornings she would grab her purse and head for the shopping center. Maybe buying something—a new dress, perhaps—would help her feel better. Lunch with a friend also helped. She hoped that when the bills came in maybe Sam wouldn't look at the itemized account.

When the first of the month came, Sam would sit down to pay the bills and flip through the charge records. He noticed the department store charges she made and seethed as he calculated the cost. Judy would usually leave the room when she saw he was working on the bills, flinching mentally as she thought of his anger. Then the yelling would start and Judy would scream back. The fight would continue until Judy cried. Sam would then quiet down and try to console her.

When all was calm again, he would say, "It's time to discuss the budget again," and Judy would agree.

The whole drama was repeated again and again with the same absurd outcome. Neither of them was able to discover why money was such an enormous problem, until they sat down together with a marriage counselor and examined what was happening.

First, they identified their main problem, which was not budgeting money but learning to satisfy each other emotionally. They learned that masked emotional needs, expressed through finances, popped out irrationally for both of them. Judy wanted Sam's love, not his money. Sam wanted security, a feeling he had never had in his life, and one that he felt Judy kept taking away from him.

Second, they planned actions to alter their situation. Sam felt he was no Valentino, but was willing in small ways to show affection—a hug, a kiss, a quiet chat. Judy felt she could live this way with him without demands for more.

Third, they still had to negotiate a budget. Judy learned to speak up for herself without automatically capitulating to Sam's suggestions. Sam learned from her that running the household was more expensive than he had thought. Both were active in negotiating a reasonable spending plan.

Fourth, they learned that bargaining is best done when each person's ideas are respected and mutual openness is present. They found that listening and understanding, as well as assertiveness, were all part of this process. Hidden agendas, deceitfulness and attempts to manipulate had prevented successful bargaining in the past. Now they were able to discuss openly any issue that arose with less heat and more light.

Fifth, they discovered that repetitious arguments meant that they were misunderstanding each other's emotional needs. At that point it was necessary for them to find the missing link in understanding and then do something about it. When they learned how to be fair to each other, they were carried beyond money problems into an enjoyable relationship.

· 5. *Build on each other's accomplishments.* There is a false dichotomy many companions establish for themselves in their life together. A stimulating career, an all-consuming hobby, a fascinating community of friends or a challenging civic project is perceived as *taking away* from one's relationship with a partner. Ultimately, such a view forces a choice between a mate and a special interest. The assumption is similar to the one established through a management training simulation exercise called the "zero-sum game," which essentially says that when there are two competing business managers, the achievement of one takes away from that of the other. Any close relationship between two people developed on this basis usually fails.

A valid, workable and fair agreement between couples today includes just the opposite—the accomplishments of either person *add to* the total enjoyment of both. It makes their union more interesting, spirited and fulfilling. Direct participation in an activity that is valued by a partner is unnecessary, but supporting his or her involvement in it is important. Unless both are supportive of each other in this area, the relationship will be marred by competition, malice and jealousy.

For a relationship to work, companions need not be equal in

achievements or abilities. It is enough that each companion feel that he or she has something to contribute to their joint happiness. This something can simply be a capacity for showing compassion, decisiveness or common sense, or the ability to nurture.

When one's only goal in life is perceived as holding on to a mate, a union becomes burdensome for both. Unless couples feel they have important sources of stimulation outside themselves, they tend to feed emotionally on one another and their relationship closes in on them in a suffocating way.

Couples who have grown apart or view their relationship as boring or impersonal do so not only because a compelling outside interest has distracted them, but because they have not allowed their self-expression to add to their *mutual* enjoyment. Pairs may have thoroughly contemporary ideas about living but archaic notions about living together. Negative conceptions of marriage as the dependency of one on the other, a burden of responsibility or entrapment prevent a couple's enjoyment of an intimate bond. An aging relationship can be viewed as dull compared with new outside excitement. Thus a couple may completely miss the pluses of living together that come with time—intimate conversations based on a rich past shared by both and mutual enjoyment of children. The false notion that a relationship prevents self-fulfillment can be reconsidered in light of the long-run benefits of intimacy.

When a couple view their relationship defensively, that is, as a closed system where outside influences are considered a threat, then their union usually wastes away. But, when a pair understand that outside interests can add to their common pleasure, then a union can prosper and grow. Nothing has to be denied or hidden. Life can be embraced enthusiastically by couples who enjoy living together and are not blinded by narrow-minded conceptions of marriage, or who use outside interests as an escape. Everyone knows that new experiences are appreciated less when not shared with someone. That someone can easily be a lifelong companion.

6. *Evaluate your contract on three levels of exchange.*
Once partners are more aware of what's involved in living with

one another, they are able to negotiate a realistic contract. By then they generally know what they like and dislike in one another, they understand differences between themselves and they have learned to communicate.

In order to determine whether or not a couple's exchanges are fair, a basis for evaluation is necessary. Looking at the essence of a satisfactory agreement helps this appraisal. The Chinese saying "One hand washes the other" expresses the essential quality for fairness. This epigram does not, of course, refer to one's habits of cleanliness. Rather, it suggests in any satisfying union both partners are able to please not only themselves but each other in a manner that is mutually beneficial.

How can this mutuality be evaluated? First, couples can assess their union at any point in time as excellent, good, mediocre or poor according to this standard of reciprocal benefits. Because satisfaction is influenced by internal developmental changes unique to adulthood, and by external circumstances relating to situational stress and changes in a pair's relationship, it varies considerably from time to time.

Second, a couple's criterion for appraising mutuality is distinctive. One pair's meat may be another pair's poison. Some wish more closeness in their relationship, while others prefer greater distance. A perfectly agreeable relationship for one pair may include excessive arguing, while another couple can tolerate only occasional quarreling. A case in point indicates the foolishness of setting a common standard for all.

A businessman visitor in Boston was walking the back streets admiring the charm of a rowhouse neighborhood when he saw a couple fighting in the backyard. The wife had a broom she adeptly used on her husband, while he retaliated with slaps to her face. Faces flushed and neck muscles bulging, they shrieked obscenities while inflicting blows on each other. The visitor ran up to the couple and valiantly held them apart. Shocked by his sudden intervention, they looked dumfounded at each other, and then, almost on cue, turned on him. A swat with a broom and a hard shove by a powerful arm sent the man scurrying into the street. Safe on neutral ground, he looked back to make certain they were not pursuing him, and quietly brushed himself off. A neighbor, who had viewed the whole spectacle from his window perch, yelled out to the man, "Hey, mister! You shouldn't have done that. Marge and Tim fight like that once a week so they can live together. They're a great pair!"

Every couple's idea of happiness is different from that of other pairs, but all can ask the same questions to evaluate mutuality on various levels of interaction. Three levels of exchange, alluded to throughout this book, can form the basis for this assessment.

1. the three r's: Are roles, responsibilities, and rituals mutually satisfying?
2. the rainbow's end: Are emotional expectations gratifying to both?
3. the hidden powerhouse: Are needs and drives acceptably matched?

Couples can discuss specific areas under each of these headings to further clarify levels of exchange:

1. the three r's: careers, household duties, finances, sex, parenting roles, friends, social activities, relatives, mealtimes and bedtimes and life style.
2. the rainbow's end: companionship, flexibility, affection, security, consideration, fairness, trust, bargaining, respect and care.
3. the hidden powerhouse: control, intimacy, dependence, passivity, independence, inclusion, assertiveness and sexuality.

This is a check list for couples to appraise fairness in their agreement. The first level, "the three r's," is heavily influenced by changes in society. It is the hotly debated public area where issues like feminine rights impinge on intimate ties. Surprisingly, it is the easiest to change when difficulties arise. Husbands and wives survive together even though a woman has a career away from home, insists that her husband help with household duties and child care, uses her maiden name and demands that she be addressed as "Ms."

The second level of exchange, "the rainbow's end," is more difficult for pairs to define. Expectations are fuzzy and are perceived differently by partners. Affectionate behavior by one may be seen as aloofness by the other. Bargaining by one may be construed as angry attacks by the other. A preposterous example highlights differences in perceived expectations. Betty H., married twenty-four years to John, insisted she only wanted a little more consideration from him. He loudly argued that he had always tried to be thoughtful and was tired of her complaints. More quarreling followed, until she was asked what she meant by "consideration." Her straight-faced response was: "I don't like him coming home and saying nothing. Since our children are gone, he could help me cook dinner when he comes in from work. Then he could wash the dishes while I relaxed. After that, I would like him to sit down and tell me about his day. I want him to talk to me! I think he could bring a gift home to me every few nights . . . maybe flowers, perfume, or sweets. That's what I would call a considerate husband." After that explanation John felt he could never live up to her expectations, and decided to give up. Obviously, both had to readjust their wishes in terms of realistic expectations that each could understand and fulfill in a satisfying way.

The third level of exchange, "the hidden powerhouse," has more to do with a couple's basic fit together. It is less amenable to change, since a pair's awareness of deep personal needs is often illusive. Needs unite people powerfully, and provide a basis for security, interdependence and caring. They are the foundation of any relationship and an underpinning for mutuality in a union. When coupling works well on this level, it is less difficult to find solutions to problems on other levels of bonding. Expectations are more easily clarified and roles are changed as needed. But all this can occur only when a pair has found a mutually gratifying level of security, interdependence and caring. This is the most substantive level of bonding that affects a couple's future.

# Checking Your Relationship

1. Are you aware of the ground rules that govern your relationship? Can you relate them to specific examples, such as defining who does which household task?
2. What meanings do you and your partner attach to fairness? How are they applicable in your relationship?
3. Have you considered the need for negotiation as your relationship changes? Can you negotiate without threatening your mutual security?
4. Do you feel that one of you gets his or her way more in your relationship? What can both of you do to make it more equitable?
5. If you wish more affection, can you coach your partner about what you want by first showing him or her by your own actions what you like? Then can you tell your partner what makes you feel loved and appreciated?
6. Do both you and your partner like to bargain in the same way? How can the process of bargaining be negotiated so that both of you feel it is fair?
7. Are you both willing to share the responsibilities of living together?
8. Do you generally consult each other on decisions that are important? What decisions do you feel are unnecessary to discuss with your partner? Is this agreeable to both of you?
9. Do you find pleasure in one another's accomplishments? Do the achievements of one or the other add to your relationship?
10. Can you evaluate your relationship on the three levels of exchange mentioned in this chapter? How do you rate it overall? What are your mutual areas of strength and weakness?

# 11

# Step Five: Free to Be Together

COUPLES ARE FOREVER IN A QUANDARY. IF THEY ARE engaged they waver about tying the knot. When they live together they can't decide about marriage. Once they're wed they're doubtful about staying together. If they're living apart they wonder whether they shouldn't get back together. Even when separated prior to divorce, they are uncertain about the final step. If divorced they are unsure of remarriage. Decisions, decisions, decisions, none of which seems easy to make.

The feeling underlying this ferment is the strong desire for personal freedom. People actually use the shopworn phrase "I want to be free" over and over again when they step inside a marriage counselor's office to discuss their troubled relationship. Tired of the conflict and sense of entrapment they feel with a mate, they wish to free themselves from their emotional binds. The obvious solution to the problem, and the one chosen more frequently today, is divorce. The mass exodus from marriage or other living-together arrangements is the result of the belief that there is more personal freedom to be found away from a close relationship with another. Yet most people still want companionship and are faced with the same doubts and discontent when they find someone new, plus having to live with a sense of failure about their previous ties.

Since anyone can get a divorce today, even though it may be experienced as a piercing personal loss and tragedy, the challenging question is whether or not partners can stay together and still find a measure of personal freedom and happiness.

## Five Ways to Personal Freedom in Living Together

*Find self-direction, not escape.* Freedom is an inspiring word to most Americans. It conjures up memories of the Continental Congress in Philadelphia, Lincoln signing the Emancipation Proclamation, civil rights marches in Washington. Most people resist confinement or bondage, even if such a life is shared with a person who supposedly is a lovemate.

However, freedom is always relative and only meaningful in comparison with some form of oppression. Absolute freedom is nihilism that does not consider the rights of others and leads to its own tyranny. Erich Fromm, in *Escape from Freedom*, wrote of the abdication of personal freedom during the rise of Nazi Germany. He saw the blind obedience of the German populace to authoritarian rule as an escape from self-determinism. Personal autonomy, he said, is not freedom from the need to make choices, to be involved, but freedom to take responsibility for oneself, to achieve self-fulfillment.

Similarly, in living together, freedom is found through self-direction and willingness to cope with the problems of intimacy, not through avoidance and escape. People continually look for panaceas outside themselves when they are not self-motivated. Some escape into marriage. Finding it intolerable to live by themselves or with their parental families, such people mistakenly think that marriage will release them from unhappiness. Others escape into divorce. The illusion of freedom is preserved by the chance to be irresponsible and carefree once again, but eventually such a life becomes boring or pointless. An impulsive divorce does not automatically bring freedom any more than a rash marriage ensures happiness.

Self-direction is not gained through external means, though a career, social causes, religion or friends may help. It is discovered through knowing enough about oneself to make responsible decisions. Furthermore, it is found more easily through close ties to another than in the freewheeling existence of single life. Even when a companion is crotchety, at least there is a point of contrast to enable one to clearly define oneself. Besides, it is nice to know that if one yells, someone will hear it and the sound will not simply bounce off the walls.

Mark and Jackie C. were married fourteen years before trouble began. Successful in separate careers, parents of three children and financially comfortable, they had all the ingredients necessary for living together with ease and happiness. But differences in temperament brought increasing friction. Mark was totally uninhibited in expressing his emotions and behaved as if he had invented the word "freedom." Jackie, who was much more controlled, allowed him his extravagances and occasional tirades, and most of the time was entertained by his histrionics. She enjoyed their quiet moments of intimacy and her rewarding job as a corporate manager gave her additional satisfaction.

Not until Mark's barbs became sharper, and his accusations about her running everything became overbearing, did their problems increase. Tired of the exhausting verbal battles, Jackie suggested they seek help. Mark was incensed—he knew more than those mealy-mouthed professionals anyway. The subject was dropped. Weeks later, after an evening with friends and ample quantities of Scotch, Mark became combative and made several vitriolic remarks. Finally Jackie could take no more and said, "Get the hell out of the house! I don't need your grief anymore. I don't want to see your face again!" He slapped her and walked out.

Legal actions quickly began. Lawyers met lawyers. Angry calls from each other left both feeling defeated. Mark was willing to seek professional help, but only if they sought it together. Although Jackie agreed, she felt it was too little and too late. Both seriously doubted that anything could be done, but still they knew they had a lot that was worth saving in their relationship. Neither felt their lives would be totally destroyed by divorce, but both told the therapist they preferred trying to work things out so that they could stay together.

How could a solution be found without relinquishing either one's autonomy? It meant giving up attitudes that prevented intimacy—Mark's bullheadedness and fierce temper, Jackie's excessive circumspection and self-control.

Bullheadedness gave way to even-handedness. Rigid self-control changed to spontaneity. Temper was modified to accommodate debate. The changes made each feel better personally. Occasionally seeing each other for dinner, going to parties together or taking the children to the park on a Sunday afternoon reassured them that warm feelings remained.

Mark was fearful that Jackie would clamp down on him—something he admitted for the first time; he was vulnerable to her moods and reactions. When she recognized this, she was compassionate toward him in a way not expressed previously. Pride became less important, and they became less willing to make all their exchanges a battle of wits.

Time passed and they were still separated. The question remained whether or not they should live together. Mark had been kicked out, and it was difficult for him to ask to return. Jackie wanted him back, but felt that his previous insults and physical abuse made it imperative that he make the first move.

As a face-saving maneuver, he drew on all his bombastic skill and said he would come back, but only if they bought a new king-size bed. She astutely agreed that their old bed was lumpy and they should have a new bed—one he chose all by himself.

Later both agreed they found more individual freedom in their intimacy than they did in the eight months of separation. Dating, quiet evenings and opportunities to go to new and exciting places had not given them the same feeling of relaxed enjoyment that being together did, once they ended the tumultuous phase of their bonding.

Self-direction comes from knowing more about yourself than you do about your companion. A partner cannot prevent self-discovery. When you invest more authority in a mate than in yourself for your happiness, he or she will inhibit your self-development. But even in this situation you can always discover avenues of self-fulfillment by developing outside interests, hobbies or your career, thus gaining the confidence to be autonomous. Only at this point can you make a responsible decision as to whether or not the relationship should be ended.

Numerous companions that separate find themselves mired in added responsibilities, fewer choices for self-fulfillment and a battle for survival, because they have not begun the process of self-discovery in marriage.

*Learn to separate without leaving.* Whether or not couples recognize it, *every* good marriage or living-together arrangement goes through several periods of emotional detachment. Changes in personal needs or self-direction force alterations in a relationship. Some pairs do not discern the true meaning of these changes and feel that their union has completely ended, when the change necessary is primarily a realignment.

Emotional distancing is essential for everyone at certain times in the normal course of living. Personal needs for privacy and aloneness can be respected by a partner without threat to a relationship.

Unions that are turbulent or suffocating are based on a fixed, rigid image of living together that allows no change and shackles both. Some partners are so inflexible that even before marriage they have fixed ideas about wedding arrangements, relations with in-laws and choice of honeymoon sites. During marriage they fight over sex, money, children and personality differences. After divorce they continue to battle over financial arrangements and child custody. Even when they remarry, their heated altercations continue and involve the new spouses. They literally fight until one or the other dies.

Here is a chilling story. The duty chaplain at Arlington National Cemetery in Washington, D. C., saw a solitary figure silhouetted against the early evening sky as he drove by. He stopped the car, got out and walked closer. He saw it was a woman with her head bowed, standing beside a new grave, and compassionately went over to speak to her. Startled, she looked up, and seeing the cross on his uniform spoke. "Chaplain, I don't need any help. This is my husband buried here. I told him sometime ago that I would see him dead and spit on his grave. I just lived up to my promise!" Then she turned and briskly walked away.

Other couples experience difficulty disengaging from one another, but not as dramatically as this wife did with her dead husband. Pairs can be bound together more forcibly by their anger than others are by their love. Paradoxical as it may seem, it is easier to gain emotional distance when caring and liking exist than when hate, guilt and fear are present.

Finding peace with a partner is comparable to finding peace with oneself. A decision about divorce can be made more responsibly when the union can be viewed with some detachment in an atmosphere free of agitation over the threat of losing one's spouse. Letting go of bitterness, inordinate disappointment and guilt, as well as the excessive fear of togetherness or aloneness, allows emotional distancing to occur in a manner both can tolerate; then a rational decision about the future can be made.

Distancing from a companion occurs in the best and worst unions and does not always have to be viewed negatively. Separate vacations, visits to friends or family out of town and other forms of separation can help both appreciate their togetherness more fully. Separation, even under duress, is *neutral*. There is a fifty-fifty chance it will lead to reuniting. Severing constricting ties through a trial separation is more hopeful than staying together and fighting it out. Separation is a tentative decision that is not tantamount to divorce.

Times of detachment can be used by couples to sort out priorities, find new interests, date one another (but not other people) and deal with responsibilities alone. Separation should be used by couples not to endlessly discuss whether or not they will reunite, but rather to settle the practical issues of living apart and have fun together whenever possible.

Couples tied too tightly together must go through an emotional disassociation before they can even decide whether or not they like one another. Only through distancing can one discover what a mate is like and what nonpossessive closeness feels like. Otherwise, the basis for contact cannot be differentiated from being stuck together. A self-directed person appreciates closeness because separateness and aloneness are known.

Grief becomes crushing at various points in the process of painful unshackling. It is not unusual for couples in marriage counseling to accuse the therapist of making their relationship worse as each seeks a measure of autonomy. Often in the final phase of severing the unhealthy part of their bonds, pairs feel that their relationship is over. On the contrary, it is precisely at this point that couples can make a decision about the future of their union based on less frantic needs to hold on, and then affirm the positive values of their relationship.

Gail Sheehy in *Passages* attributes the distancing that occurs between couples to maturational drives around the age of thirty when a pair has been married approximately seven years. The stereotypical husband seeks renewed self-direction and pushes his traditional homemaker wife into doing the same. While both are seeking more individual direction, each wants the other to remain constant. Pushing with one hand, they hold on tightly with the other. All this conflict between tugging and holding tight Sheehy calls the Catch-30 dilemma. But this occurs not only at the age of thirty but at any age when a relationship becomes constricting. And for some pairs it happens more than once. Anytime one's needs for another become overbearing, distancing is necessary. This distancing can result in modifications that enable a couple's relationship to be more enjoyable.

A relationship works simply because both partners *want* it to work. Distancing is a natural part of letting your union breathe. When couples have found a rhythm of distancing and closeness at various times, their union can more easily survive. Closeness comes only to those who know what it means to be separate individuals.

*Deal with emotional binds practically.* Personal freedom has less to do with one's marital status than with one's state of mind. Singleness does not free a person any more than marriage entraps an individual, despite folklore to the contrary.

Inner chains are more restrictive than external constraints. If that were not so, Alexander Solzhenitsyn, incarcerated in a Soviet prison camp, would never have had the inner freedom to write his novel chronicling the grimness of prison life. Nor would William Shakespeare have written so movingly about kings and queens who, with all their power, still suffered agonies of inner turmoil and despair.

When a couple is immobilized by indecision about their destiny together, there are several courses of action that can be taken. Fleeing a relationship without so much as a good-bye to a partner is the least acceptable course. Giving a partner an ultimatum to either stay or get out is usually not a good idea, either. Final decisions are not readily made in thirty seconds, and, anyway, even if they were, few are able to follow through on them. There are more positive ways to break the bind of indecision.

A characteristic of uncertainty is ambivalence. Couples doubting their relationship often live with one foot firmly planted inside, and the other foot just as securely anchored outside. Which way does one go and how is a decision made?

Whereas some pairs act impulsively, others go on for years debating both sides of the question—like medieval theologians trying to decide how many angels fit on the head of a pin. In *Scenes from a Marriage*, Ingmar Bergman has his couple, Johan and Marianne, confronting each other endlessly through marriage, divorce and even remarriage to others, always trying to determine their fate together.

Many companions carry on in a similar way. Because they never fully commit themselves to a course of action, they suffer intense pain. Couples have shifted a hundred and eighty degrees in the last twenty years in their personal hopes for a relationship—from expecting to live happily ever after to assuming that the only happy ending is a sad one.

Partners do not have to be mired in indecision indefinitely. They can experiment with tentative conclusions that test the most positive direction to follow. For example, if one partner wants marriage and the other has doubts and a period of living together does not indicate a clear decision, then setting a definite date for marriage, making practical arrangements, and then living *as if* their relationship is going to be permanent will force a decision. At worst, the relationship will break up at some point in this process, but the pain will be no greater than at the earlier stage of indecision.

If one partner wants a divorce and the other does not, a trial separation may be an intermediate step. Settling realistic necessities, contacting lawyers and living as singles for a mutually agreed-upon time will help test the idea. Then an evaluation can be made to decide the permanent outcome.

On the other hand, if a pair has been behaving for years toward each other as if their relationship is doomed, then a mutual decision to reverse the direction for a specific period of time can be made. Then they can behave toward each other more hopefully—for a pleasant change—and a realistic decision can follow, based on their success in living together during this discrete period of time.

For couples who feel the necessity of making total and complete commitments to one another but are tired of the demands this makes on them, a decision to live together more casually, without trying so hard to make the relationship work, can help them decide the outcome of their union. Options like these, which do not force immediate closure, can more easily help couples to determine the future of their relationship. These short intervals of mutually agreed-upon experimentation provide a basis for beginning anew or finally ending the relationship.

Any direction that offers the most *hope* for the two individuals involved is the best one to follow. Companions do not have to be sad forever. They can even "live happily ever after" in this despairing decade.

*Develop interests.* It is difficult for marriage or any living-together arrangement to sustain itself today primarily as a lonely-hearts club. Each partner must be self-sufficient. This does not mean that one cannot seek a mate's support and protection but that such closeness is not enough to keep a relationship alive.

Each companion must find fulfillment and freedom through pursuing his or her own interests. One is lucky when a career coincides with self-expression, but that is not usually the case. Surveys and research reports indicate that over 75 percent of America's workers are dissatisfied with their jobs. Women have moved in increasing numbers to occupations outside the home, but they are not necessarily happier. In general, their satisfaction comes from indirect benefits—meeting new friends, feeling useful and making money—rather than from the job itself.

Expressing oneself through hobbies, recreational activities, life styles and volunteer work is usually more gratifying than working to earn money. Increased leisure time makes this possible. With a little imagination, creativity and appreciation for novelty, couples can find interests that absorb them and make their lives together more interesting.

Partners can support each other's self-expression and do everything possible to enhance it. But that requires giving up the traditional mentality about home and family living. Men can no longer view freedom solely as their evenings out with "the boys" while women guard home and hearth, imprisoned by responsibility and sameness. Children must be a joint responsibility and an expression of both partners' interests. Women have as much need to feel free as men do, even when they choose to be a housewife and mother. Providing opportunities, both at home and away from it, for each to have periods of freedom from responsibility is necessary for a healthy partnership. The key is flexibility and a willingness to be influenced by the other's needs.

*Learn to live with endings and beginnings.* Change is a way of life for most people today. The farmer turned businessman was not just speaking sentimentally when he said he missed the good old days: "It used to be that I could put on the same overalls, do the same chores and come in from the fields at sunset and relax. Now I have to decide which clothes to wear, when to service my car, where to eat lunch, what contacts to make, when to finish my paperwork and when to come home. I liked it better when I didn't have to make so many decisions and things were simpler."

Our speeded-up existence today often seems like the kaleidoscopic slapstick antics of the Keystone Kops of the silent movies. Too many choices and too much freedom can be as hampering as a life that is too constricting. The upshot is that today people are faced with more opportunities for significant endings and beginnings than were encountered in previous generations.

A middle-aged mother is obsolete to her grown children and must confront a new life. An organization man is thrown off the career ladder and decides to open his own business. Career changes force people back to school to learn new vocations. Leaving old friends and surroundings is necessary to start a new life in a strange city. Experimenting with different life styles requires changes in personal habits. Changing partners creates stress through divorce and remarriage. Even living with the same companion for ten, twenty or thirty years indicates that periodic modifications are necessary.

All these personal changes profoundly affect the quality of intimate relationships today. A partner who continually discusses an ex-spouse, even in a derisive way, has not let go of the past. A spouse who is plagued by guilt and a sense of failure from a previous relationship is only partially available to a new companion. A mate that is overly cautious and fearful with a different partner is likewise holding on to the past. Even husbands and wives married for years who feel that they have grown apart, or that their relationship is boring, are living together on outdated emotions.

The essential point is that emotions between pairs must be kept *current*. Bonds between a man and woman are malleable. They can withstand a lot of banging around that comes with quarreling, misunderstanding, separations or individual changes. But they cannot survive continued neglect. When important feelings are tied to an ex-spouse, a notion about the permanency of a first love, or children and careers without regard for a partner, then relations become strained and unhappy, and ultimately will kill the union.

Today's rash of marital breakdown among couples married twenty, twenty-five or thirty years can be partially explained by the discrepancy between the attitudes of yesterday and the reality of today. Back in the forties and fifties it was assumed that one would marry, hang the notion of idealized love on a peg and go one's merry way. Permanency and exclusiveness were taken for granted—a major mistake, as many later realized. Today marriage is a more complicated institution. There is less tolerance for boring, uninteresting or unequal relationships, since companions expect a higher degree of intimacy, as well as freedom to pursue outside interests. Moreover, depersonalization and loneliness in other areas of living often make one's personal ties more important.

Feelings between two people must be kept contemporary and alive. Developing satisfying patterns of communication and expressing continued concern for one another help this process. Learning to enjoy living together rather than simply tolerating one another, or seeing a union primarily as a duty, also strengthens a couple's bonds.

It is also important to adapt to endings and beginnings that occur. Endings mean giving up stale emotions tied to ideals of marriage no longer viable, an outdated perception of a partner or a life style that has changed because career goals have been achieved and children have grown and left home. New beginnings are possible for couples only through endings—something many pairs fail to recognize. Whatever the set of circumstances may be that creates hopelessness for a pair, it does not always mean a relationship has ended. There is a choice to be made. Each can consider whether or not a new and more promising beginning is possible. For two who have lived together for years it is often easier to start over together. Like purifying metal by burning the dross away, couples find better levels of closeness after undergoing a series of trials.

Fears prevent some couples from coping with endings and beginnings. Fear of change, of losing a mate or of staying together forever immobilizes them for years. Often, to break the stranglehold of these nameless demons, one must face the ultimate fear, death. Denying it, fighting it unreasonably, or fearing it continually only makes living intolerable. Reminding oneself of this universal and inescapable human experience can give a different perspective on living together. Fearing the loss of a companion often means that the fear of death has not been squarely faced. Endings and beginnings are easier to confront when one knows that the most that can be expected from a partner is companionship that is essentially transitory. Shared memories, adventures and good times are comforting, and will mitigate the loneliness of dying alone.

Facing endings and beginnings together is a profound part of every durable union. Stagnation is less likely when partners encounter these changes in a manner that allows both to grow and develop. In fact, the only certain death sentence to any relationship is a decision not to change.

# Checking Your Relationship

1. Under what circumstances do you feel the greatest sense of inner freedom? With your partner? Alone? Are there ways to improve your personal sense of freedom together?
2. Are you bothered by fears that threaten your relationship as a couple? Can you discuss these with one another and find a mutually satisfying sense of security together?
3. Can you recall experiences in your relationship when it felt as if it had ended, when all that was needed was only a readjustment to each other?
4. Do you consider separate vacations a threat to your relationship? Do you think holidays should be spent together as a couple or family?
5. What would you do with yourself if you had a week alone without your partner?
6. What are the significant endings and new beginnings you and your partner have shared together? Did they isolate you from each other or draw you closer together?
7. What changes in your personal life forced some kind of readjustment with your partner?
8. Do you and your partner have a sense of what you want from life both separately and together? Do your private desires conflict with your mutual wishes as a couple? Do you and your partner understand the conflicts between your private and mutual goals? How can you be more successful in resolving them?
9. Under what circumstances do you and your companion feel more freedom together?
10. What makes living together most worthwhile for you?

# 12

## It's Closer than You Think

A YOUNG BOY WAS AT THE BREAKFAST TABLE WITH HIS father on a leisurely Sunday morning. The boy asked the father, "Where is God?" Happy to give his son a lesson in theology, the father said, "Everywhere."

"Is God on the moon?"

"Yes."

"Is He on earth?"

"Certainly." The father said, burying his head in the Sunday papers.

"Is He in Russia?"

The father simply nodded.

"Is He in Japan?"

He nodded again.

"Is He in America?"

Another nod.

"Is He in Missouri?"

This time the father looked up—they lived in St. Louis, and he wondered what his son had in mind. "Yes," he said firmly.

"Is He in St. Louis?"

"Yes."

"Is God in our neighborhood?" Irritably the father said, "Yes, yes, yes."

"Is He in our house?"

"Certainly," the father said with an air of piety.

"Is He in this room?"

The father suddenly felt trapped but managed to say convincingly, "Yes."

Looking around the room as if spooked by a ghost, the child continued, "Is He at this table?" The trapped feeling grew more intense as the father said, "Without a doubt." The son lifted the lid of the sugar bowl and said, "Is He in here?" Disturbed at his son's idea of God, the father said, "Yes." Excited, the boy quickly slammed down the lid on the sugar bowl and said "*Gotcha!*"

The story of intimacy between a man and woman is somewhat like the above anecdote. The essence of closeness is everywhere but nowhere at the same time. When one grasps for it, it slips away. But if the relationship is sound, it appears spontaneously and unexpectedly.

For most partners intimacy is closer than they think. In fact, it is present during the entire lifetime of a union in varying degrees of intensity, and can be found whenever partners stop to recognize it—in moments of romantic passion, simply enjoying one another's company or sharing open communication.

## Discover the Necessary Conditions for Intimacy That Fit You

No description of intimacy fits every couple, since each union is different from any other, but there are conditions that all close relationships must meet—at least to some degree—if they are to be successful.

*When couples cease trying to contain closeness, it emerges spontaneously.* Intimacy is not a commodity, backed by a money-back guarantee, that comes with a marriage license. It cannot be taken for granted when it exists, but neither can one pressure the other when it does not. Clamoring for closeness only kills it. Trying to hold on to it can make it stale and formal. But enjoying it when it comes unprompted in a caring relationship makes living together rewarding.

*Intimacy is neither constant nor suffocating.* It is possible to have too much closeness, surprising as that may seem. The small child who found the wounded bird, and whose tiny hands squeezed it too tightly while loving it, discovered that he smothered it unintentionally. Likewise, when couples hold on to one another too tightly, they restrict one another's initiative and self-direction, and eventually kill the desire to be together.

*When unrealistic expectations cease, closeness comes.* A wife berated her husband for never listening, but he *was* listening to her. A husband complained that his mate was unaffectionate, but sitting next to him she was quietly stroking his hand. A couple decided to divorce after years of bitterness; the night this decision was made they spent the evening together enjoying moments of tenderness, including a memorable sexual experience. The irony of such situations is frequent in the lives of most couples. To a pair's surprise, puzzlement or even dismay, they often find what they want when they cease expecting it. In an ongoing relationship, if two people approach a problem in the spirit of friendliness, they may be surprised by the happy consequences.

*No longer dreaming dreams, companions will find the present sufficient and intimate.* Dreams give rise to hope, but unfulfilled dreams produce disappointment and frustration, which can corrode a union. But when the realization comes that it is enough to take a partner at face value, with all his or her flaws, a first step has been taken toward contentment in the relationship, and quiet pleasures will naturally follow. Once accomplished, the rest is easy.

*If living together is simplified, closeness emerges frequently.* No one likes to think of himself or herself as being simpleminded; there is more status to being complex and enigmatic. But it helps to approach living together with a bit of simplemindedness. Everything does not have to be worrisome, knotty or difficult. To avoid chaos and confusion, a pair must be willing to search for the simplest and most direct solutions to their problems.

*Closeness emerges when fears evaporate—including fears of losing one another.* Fears cripple and deplete companions and separate them from their potential. They are the supreme frustrator of human hope. Named and nameless fears are the real cancer in living together. The fear of abandonment keeps

many partners on tenterhooks much of the time they are together. Facing this enemy in oneself head-on is the only
remedy possible. Until it is conquered, intimacy has no meaning.

*Emotional equality ensures intimacy.* When one treats his or
her partner as an equal, because the same feelings and needs
are shared, then one has learned a basic lesson of intimacy. As
long as both can transcend their personal and sexual differences
in this manner, they can find enough communion to keep them
together. Closeness is difficult to find from a competitive, inferior or superior position.

*Intimacy is being able to move away from a partner.* Physical
proximity does not ensure intimacy. Some couples spend their
time together arguing about why more time is not spent being
together—so they can argue about their times apart. Closeness
comes when two people are always available to each other in a
deeply personal sense; the communication of a word, a touch,
a shared experience, a longing or a funny incident is enough. It
follows the natural contour of bonding and can be found
whether partners are physically together, or apart.

*When each knows enough about the other, closeness can be
immediate.* What makes one tick? Knowing the answer to that
question about one another comes with time spent in living
together. Weaknesses are tolerated or accepted. Strengths are
respected and reinforced. Differences are viewed without threat.
Both have a sense of the possibilities and limits of living together. Neither continually overreacts to the idosyncrasies of
the other, but can tolerate them, even if not always graciously.
It is easier to feel tenderness toward someone known and
trusted even when the knowing means being aware of de-
ficiences.

*Intimacy can be found through light-hearted experiences to-
gether.* It is impossible to live as a couple without a sense of
humor. The absurd and idiotic things that happen must be
laughed about, because humor has a way of breaking up the
tension of living. Couples with children are fortunate indeed.
Childish antics often make parents laugh and help to draw
them together. Sometimes it is easier for a couple to untie
knotty problems after they have had a light-hearted experience
together.

*Intimacy follows more easily once mutual ground rules for living together are established.* When a couple have not revealed their separate assumptions for a relationship to each other and thereby developed a mutual commitment, their relationship often goes awry. Forging a joint agreement through revealing separate expectations aids the process of commitment. Then knowing where one stands with the other allows love feelings to grow and flourish.

*As the balance of living together begins to work, intimacy becomes more visible.* Companions develop a sense of balance in their relationship through giving and receiving and sharing responsibilities. Though affected by the birth of children, career challenges, the aging process, unexpected crises or new directions in life style, the balance remains in a good relationship to keep each linked to the other.

*If a union has proved its worth, closeness exists even if it is not clearly evident.* Many couples sell their union short. They have come through turbulence and difficult transitions without acknowledging their triumphs. Maybe a bit battered from the struggle, uneasy about the calm or holding on to old patterns of behavior that are no longer needed, they continue to plow through their self-created morass. Letting go of the obsolete—the stifling hold of unnecessary needs—allows each to bask freely in the warm sunlight of an enjoyed relationship. The past habits of worry, depression, fear, anger, frustrated dreams and unimportant jealousies can be discarded to make room for favorable experiences together.

*After couples encounter struggles with each other, closeness surfaces.* For some the road to intimacy is filled with potholes and detours. There are periodic threats of divorce, temporary separations or vicious attacks before they reach a quiet warm spot of kindness. They can adjust their turbulent bonding only through arguing or quarreling. For such couples, crusty defenses are penetrated only through confrontation. Intimacy comes only in this circuitous manner for those whose sensibilities are otherwise impenetrable.

*Intimacy follows when quarreling is no longer threatening.* Every intimate tie gets kinked at times. Successful partners learn to remove these tangles through bickering. Conflict does not necessarily mean that a relationship is over or that divorce is imminent. Reuniting after the air has been cleared of frustration and anger often means a reaffirmation of the union's strength.

*Intimacy is being less cautious or self-conscious about one's vulnerabilities in living with a partner.* Everybody has limitations, although some spend a lifetime trying to hide them. Intimacy is impossible for those unwilling to disclose their humanness. One cannot always be the perfect lover, the rational partner, the knowledgeable mate, but some partners insist on having a superior image, however impossible it may be to maintain it. Taking pride in one's completeness or even incompleteness only leads to trouble in living together. But real self-exposure leads to closeness with a trusted companion.

*Enjoying and appreciating differences in each other allow closeness to follow.* Satisfaction in living together comes easier when two have acknowledged their distinct personalities and feel little need to obliterate this uniqueness. A liberating interdependency replaces binding dependency. This knowledge, that one has a partner different from oneself, is a more authentic basis for coming together as a couple.

*When hidden desires are legitimized, closeness is also discovered.* Once a pair is able to recognize the deepest longings and wishes in each other, their union will be on a surer footing. Such knowledge makes it possible to negotiate expectations with relative ease and find a more substantial basis for intimacy.

*Being psychologically available to the other lets intimacy develop.* Companions are self-centered even in the best relationships. Most of the time one is preoccupied with one's own interests, concerns, worries or goals. But occasionally a partner must show a willingness to put aside personal cares long enough to hear about those of a partner. Everyone yearns for another to listen, to really understand. The catharsis of talking to a caring listener is not only cleansing but gives one a whole new perspective on the problem at hand. When partners are habitually able to make self-disclosures to one another, uncharted channels of intimacy are opened.

*When negativism ceases to be a way of life, closeness brings solidarity.* These are people for whom living together is a series of catastrophes. Cars break down, lawn mowers don't work, accidents happen regularly to each partner. Anxiety and emotional upset are a way of life. Misunderstanding is common. Companions spend all their energy mending their belongings and their psyches, since nothing goes right. They are in despair even before the next disaster befalls them.

The culprit is contagious negative attitudes that become self-fulfilling. These partners are defeated even before the battle begins. To change the directions of such lives, companions must first learn to support one another and find confidence in themselves in order to minimize the negativism that is weakening their relationship.

*Communication must be transparent in intimate exchanges.* Guarded, awkward or smoke-screen talking creates distance between companions. The best communication is based on self-revealing statements that are forthright. When exchanges are confused or cloaked in double meanings, there can be no real communication. As couples feel less need to hide, withhold or withdraw, they are able to create a climate conducive to closeness. Openness does not preclude privacy, which can be respected all the more because being together has become so rewarding.

*When each can count on the other always to be there in some way, closeness is present.* No one escapes life's disappointments, small or large. The sharing of these moments, no matter how distressful or ultimately inconsequential, is an eloquent part of living together. Times of anguish drive some couples apart. Either afraid of giving wordless support or making it difficult to give encouragement, partners fail to pool their strengths in periods of sorrow. They make the act of giving support unnecessarily complicated. If a partner is crying, just giving him or her a piece of Kleenex can be the right thing to do. When frustration overwhelms, simply listening sympathetically can be enough. These simple acts of kindness seal the bonds between companions.

*Intimacy need not be striven for when each partner is proud of the bond.* Ask a happily married couple how they did it, and usually they are unable to answer the question. Like a quarterback's comments after the game on what made his team win, what such a couple will say doesn't always make sense. Was it luck, skill in personal relations, knowledge or intuition? Yes, it was all that and more. Mostly spontaneously, but sometimes in a calculated way, some couples piece together their lives in such a way that the union becomes a unique work of art. Such couples simply want their relationship to work, because they are proud of it.

*When a relationship has been tested and still survives, intimacy is appreciated more fully.* No couple goes an entire lifetime together without suffering some strain on their relationship. The stress may be minor, or it may result in a lengthy separation. Misunderstanding, alienation and anger are part of this testing. Partners whose relationship endures are forced to choose one another over and over again. They do so on the basis of a better knowledge of each other and realistic appraisal of the union's possibilities. The resulting intimacy is fully appreciated, since it has been strongly tested.

*Being sensitive to each other's feelings and needs is a sign of intimacy.* Some would overwhelm their mates with ridiculous solicitousness over a hangnail. Although occasionally this kind of doting is enjoyed, more often it becomes annoying. At the other extreme, to make light of the condition of a mate bedridden with a perforated ulcer is a putdown of the worst sort. A sensitive partner appreciates the feelings of the other, whether or not such feelings are foreign to him or her. Conversely, the partner who tells a mate, "You can't understand my pain because you've never been through this," is as insensitive as the companion who overdoses with kindness or minimizes real suffering. Each does not have to go through the same pain or joy to be able to empathize with the other.

*When aloneness does not panic a partner, closeness can be found.* Learning to be alone, to lick one's own wounds in private at times, are the only paths to finding the quality—not the mere quantity—of true closeness. The strength of a couple's union is tested by their capacity to accept aloneness. Pairs cannot feel the warm touch of intimacy unless they know what separateness is like.

*If sexual fulfillment comes naturally, intimacy is known.* As closeness becomes more customary, it is easier to let sex express one's tenderness. Only those who package sex under one label, even if it is the noble label of love, find it difficult to enjoy it. When all the moods of intimacy are not allowed, then the possibilities of sexual pleasure are limited. A gentle kiss, a warm embrace, a playful slap or an aggressive advance can all express one's sensuality and either be an end in themselves or lead to sexual intercourse. Flexibility with one another and respect for each other's needs are paramount to sexual fulfillment. Sex then becomes a natural expression of intimacy for couples.

*When reduced to the lowest common denominator, intimacy is available when one decides that despite all the union's imperfections what is enjoyed together is sufficient.* Intimacy is limited for many, and is never available in a perfect state. Rather than searching for the impossible, appreciating present moments together makes it possible to find satisfaction with a mate. When partners recognize this truth, their relationship becomes more comfortable and thus more durable.

*Intimacy comes through the continuity of a joint life.* Continuity can provide a base for growth and a creative expression of one's self not found in other ways. A sense of history is gained in an abiding union and is often expressed through one's children. Intimacy takes on various shades of meaning as two pass through epochal changes in their lives together. An enduring closeness is still possible for companions even in a world that seems to be falling apart.

## Checking Your Relationship

1. Can you remember the circumstances under which you and your partner felt the closest together? Make a list of these for yourself, and have your partner do the same. Then compare the lists and check how they agree or disagree.

2. Do you and your partner agree on the quality and quantity of closeness you share? How can this be made more equitable for both of you?

3. As far as you are concerned, what prevents the easy access of closeness in your relationship? Does your partner agree? Are there ways this can be improved?

4. Is simply being together satisfying to both of you?

5. What would you like to see changed in your relationship that will improve the quality of intimacy you and your partner share together?

6. Do you allow your sense of responsibility, with all the tasks to be done, prevent you from enjoying your partner?

7. Can you and your partner plan a weekend together that will help both of you find more satisfaction as a couple?

8. Do you feel your commitment to each other has grown, is about the same, or has deteriorated gradually? If the answer is negative, can anything be done to improve the relationship?

9. What kinds of things have you and your partner never done together which you would enjoy doing? Is there any practical way for your dreams to come true?

10. Does your effort to be close to your partner seem worth it to you? If not, what do you think is the root of the problem?

# III

# Lasting Intimacy

# 13

# Children:
# Our Hope for
# the Future

THE RUDIMENTS OF INTIMACY ARE FOUND IN THE NURSERY.
Tender care, cuddling and cooing, noisy and quiet play, warm
hugs and soft words are the first experiences of closeness. Intimacy in marriage stems from this simple beginning. It is only
natural, then, for a couple who has discovered closeness together
to want to express it through creating new life.

Even when unwanted or unplanned, children are lasting and
tangible evidence of a pair's relationship. Bonds are sealed for a
lifetime through children. They outlive divorce and often even
parents themselves. They are symbols of what could have been,
what is or what shall be.

## How Children Keep Intimacy
## Alive for Parents

Children are natural bearers of gifts that are all the more
precious because they are intangible. They give adults a spontaneous and untarnished view of intimacy. Years after they are
grown and gone, parents can remember incidents that bring a
smile to their faces and a warm feeling inside.

*Youngsters help parents recognize their human foibles.*
Dr. Spock and the myriad of child-behavior books notwithstand-

ing, infants still puzzle, baffle and confuse parents. Complicated problems are continually raised by these innocents: "Why is the sky blue?" "How did all the water get in the ocean?" "Why doesn't Jamie like me?" "Why can't I make a tree in my room?" The riddles become more troublesome as they grow older. "Why can't I get a girlfriend?" "What's wrong with smoking marijuana?" "Why can't I drink when you do?" "Why won't you let me stay out later?" "I don't want to go to college, I want to be a bum!" "Susan has a Corvette, why can't I have one?" "What's wrong with staying overnight with Billy?"

To put humans in their place, God must have decided He would let them reproduce themselves and let the little devils harass the big people. Children teach parents, if nothing else, that there is no such thing as a perfect human being. These guileless souls are quick to remind parents of their inconsistencies, unfairness and even dishonesty. They can naïvely walk into difficult situations and instantly dispel the tension, reduce angry parents to tears or laughter, and sometimes offer obvious solutions to problems that parents find confusing.

They also bring responsible order to parents' lives. Vacations must be arranged around school holidays. Car pooling, PTA meetings and special children's events keep parents busy. Health needs remind parents what is necessary to maintain soundness of body and mind.

Even at an early age they follow their "Why can't I?" with the challenge "You can't stop me." That truth becomes poignant as they grow older, and all too soon parents learn they can't —and, indeed, shouldn't—stop them from doing as they wish. Parents eventually work themselves out of a job.

Thus children give parents firsthand knowledge of every stage in the growth of a living being. Parents who know they can't hold on to them forever, or force them to be something they are not, have discovered the meaning of nonpossessive and freeing closeness with their children.

*Children give parents an opportunity to do something together.* It takes a male and a female to create life. But more important, it takes these same people to nurture and civilize this new life. Early parenthood is chaotic and tends to separate partners initially. No longer able to go out when they wish, be together as they like or feel free as they once were, they are torn apart by this third party. Resentment is often felt toward the intruder who has spoiled their peaceful companionship.

Nonetheless, equilibrium is eventually restored. Parents can be flexible, almost as resilient as the tiny bit of life they brought into the world. Sensible parents recognize that joint efforts in raising children are necessary, and that mutual support protects both from the voracious demands of infants.

Parents feel they must present a united front to their progeny, and not only united but consistent. Trying to maintain both these attitudes simultaneously often creates difficulties. When they follow their instinctive common sense, rather than the way they think they should be, they soon recognize that a consistent united front is unworkable. They realize that parents can give youngsters two different personal views of life—a plus for children. Parents do not have to use the same methods of discipline or treat their children similarly in all ways. However, respect for each other's approach to parenthood is necessary, as well as a willingness to bolster each other, even though one may disagree with the other's tactics.

Children suffer only when one parent polarizes his position against that of the other parent and both effectively neutralize their influence. Youngsters then must fend for themselves, since each parent has made the other powerless. However, when parents cooperate, letting each maintain his or her own position of strength, then difficulties with children are easier to handle and children feel the strong support of parents who respect each other's opinions.

Furthermore, parents are not always consistent with their youngsters, and in fact do not have to be. Parents can grow, change and learn to be more effective. They can even be influenced by their children's desires and needs and modify their attitudes accordingly. Youngsters also learn that their parents are influenced by moods, and are not always the law enforcers they claim to be.

The only two essentials of effective parenting are a balanced mixture of firmness and tenderness on each parent's part. In other words, it helps children to experience both justice and mercy. Firmness teaches youngsters boundaries and basically strengthens their desire to grow up, even though they may complain about restrictions. Tenderness allows a child to know the meaning of intimacy within his family and then to thrive on this closeness.

It is unfortunate when one parent usually administers justice and the other shows only mercy. The first is seen as an ogre and the latter as an easy mark. Since usually neither parent enjoys the role of disciplinarian, both parents can agree to participate in setting fundamental limits for their children. Then both can likewise find times for fun and play with them. Collaboration by parents makes this possible and allows each to shift roles without being pegged as strictly the enforcer or the softie.

Though traditionally mothers have been primarily responsible for children, numerous fathers have more patience and capacity for nurturing than some mothers. Parents that cooperate on child rearing allow each to do what he or she is best suited for as a parent. Continuing the blend of firmness and tenderness, each parent can make use of special abilities, which will be appreciated more fully by the other if neither accuses the other of being ineffective. Child rearing is still a mutual task.

Children give parents the opportunity to do something together. Though traditionalists have felt it is the singular task of women, two people are really needed to raise one child. Even divorced couples often maintain joint emotional support of their children.

*The young force parents to grow up.* Responsibility in a family is often a hot potato. Children and parents alike want to keep passing it around. Needless to say, the major responsibility falls on parents by virtue of their age and standing in the family. Parents are thus restricted from acting impulsively or capriciously. They must always consider the needs of offspring. This one fact of life permanently changes a couple's entire outlook on living in a way childless pairs never experience. Their life space suddenly includes others. They have moved permanently into another plane of living, whether or not they were prepared for it, truly desired it or considered how it would change their lives. In parenthood, adulthood is important for both partners.

However, countless generations of people—even those without emotional maturity—have made it through parenthood successfully.

Parenthood can be an unusually humanizing experience. To change diapers, feed hungry mouths, wipe teary eyes, wash dirty faces and soothe scraped knees is to be reminded every day what is basic to living. The home becomes a place for all kinds of drama—funny, touching, even tragic—that are as important as anything happening in the adult world. Parents learn more about other people and themselves through a child's viewpoint.

*Offspring permit parents to be children again.* Playing in a park with their youngsters, enjoying a birthday or sharing in the surprises at Christmas gives parents a feeling of unbridled freedom and a happy sense of a return to childhood. Within comfortable boundaries, child's play can be thoroughly enjoyed by both parents and youngsters. Children provide the spontaneity and impetus, and parents can participate vicariously or directly. When play and fun are openly allowed for all family members, an important basis for closeness is found.

However, a parent that stays with children constantly is in danger of entering fantasyland full time. Another adult is needed to rescue such a parent from the lure of infantilism. With two parents raising children, one can at least periodically remind the other that both are adults. This is not to say that parents should not occasionally join in the fun, because unless they do, parenthood can be heavy and unrewarding. Play, fun and humor are always the first steps toward removing barriers between parents and children. Without intervals of lighthearted togetherness, parents will be polarized against their offspring in a manner that breeds unhappiness.

However, when parents become too much like children, roles are reversed and youngsters become parents reminding them that they must stop quarreling, acting childish or misbehaving in ways they feel are wrong. Children can sometimes be severe critics.

When parents are unhappy or argue all the time, they spoil their offspring's opportunity to be children. Youngsters will either try to be peacemakers or go the opposite direction and outdo their parents through rebellion. Troubled adolescents often say they wish their parents would stop acting like kids and grow up.

When children take over parental functions, they can be harsh taskmasters, often more tough-minded than the parents themselves. They insist that their parents stop arguing, become angry when they separate or divorce and tenaciously hold them to promises made to reform their actions. Fortunately, such situations occur only when parents completely lose their grip on their adulthood.

*Children give parents hope.* Optimism and idealism uniquely belong to the young. As yet untested, a youngster has the energy, enthusiasm and confidence to tackle tasks parents feel are impossible. A young child will think nothing of attempting tasks that require skills that even an adult may not have.

Many parents wish to give their children every advantage they themselves did not have in growing up. Hope keeps them working toward the goals they feel are indispensable for their children's welfare. Youth means opportunity, and parents do not wish to deprive their children of any opportunities they might seek, even if a child has already failed several times.

Parents have a personal investment in the future through their children. Public education, government, health services, human relations, careers, religion and political ideologies have special meaning for parents; children bring all of society's ills, as well as its benefits, into the home and force parents to confront them. It is difficult for well-meaning parents to be anything less than responsible citizens.

Parents usually think twice before ending a bad marriage, and when they do divorce, are willing to be more civilized toward each other for the sake of the children. The wishes of children can persuade parents to try to work out their marital difficulties. Sometimes this is enough encouragement for couples to change the direction of their union.

Children also keep parents tied to other family members, especially grandparents. Closer extended family ties are fitting when there are children, especially if grandparents and other relatives have established a special place of importance within a family. Generations are linked through these ties, and this continuity gives family members a sense of belonging to a tightly knit kinship system.

Although children can certainly be a burden at times—as can grandparents with their expectations—both generations give parents a link with the past and future. Loneliness and hopelessness are less likely, even when kin are not always appreciated. Buttressing one's individual existence through contact with extended family ties keeps hope alive for all concerned.

## How Parents Keep Intimacy Alive for Children

Children do not owe their parents love or any other positive emotion. As in any other close relationship, feelings must flow uncontrolled. What is given and received by either child or parent is done through respect and fondness, with a parent often initiating the exchange. This unsettling fact dawns on both parents and youngsters at some point in their ever-changing relationship.

Parents eventually realize that they have raised their children to be on their own, and that they cannot expect an emotional return on this investment. A parent's love which freely allows a child to grow up and leave is the closest to selfless caring most humans experience.

*Parents can show children what it means to be happy.* More important than financial security, nurturing concern or answers to each and every problem, the most consequential gift parents can give children is the knowledge that they as parents are happy people—happy not in the sense of a cheerful optimism impervious to real problems but in the comprehensive feeling that life can be faced with all its wonders and misfortunes by drawing on inner strength. This is a gift children will remember a lifetime because it will color their own outlook.

Contentment breeds contentment, and although parents

cannot make their children happy by whatever they do for them, at least they can give them the opportunity to grow up knowing that their parents made it as self-assured people. Children find it difficult to become adults, live their own lives or do as they wish if they know their parents are unhappy. This is why the greatest contribution parents can make to children is an affirmation of life that enables them to become untroubled and confident adults.

When grown children are faced with difficult problems or overwhelmed by doubt or despondency, the memory of parents who embraced life enthusiastically, whether in poverty or affluence, is often the deciding factor that encourages them to live productively and make wise decisions. Nothing can substitute for this inner security, and although children may find it without the aid of parents, absorbing this intimate stability from cherished parents gives them a head start in life.

Few people attain this kind of self-acceptance in living, and fewer realize it as a married couple, as shown by the divorce rates in the country today. Accepting oneself realistically yet securely, while being aware of one's imperfections, is indeed a remarkable accomplishment. Yet most of us have met people in all walks of life who make us realize it is possible.

Parents who develop inner happiness together through mutual support are able to maintain continuity in their relationship and pass it on to children as a solid base for starting life.

*Offspring receive a realistic view of life from their parents.* Afraid to punish their children or feeling guilty about disliking them at times, parents sometimes feign love and overindulge them to maintain the image of "good" parents. What parents need to remember is that it is still acceptable to discipline children, even to the extent of giving them an occasional spanking for a misdeed.

Disciplining children takes many forms, but probably the most effective methods used are removing privileges and letting them realize the natural consequences of their behavior. Short of allowing physical harm, there are many things that parents can let a child learn by himself. For example, if a toy or article of clothing is lost, the child learns he no longer has access to it. If he is late for school, then he must deal with school policy and a teacher's irritation. When he misspends an allowance, he doesn't have funds for other pleasures. When parents allow their children to suffer the natural consequences of their behavior, as adults are forced to do, they more easily become self-directed and develop values that will be helpful to them in the future.

A built-in aid for parents in helping children to grow up is the child's natural desire to please parents. Discipline and encouragement are easier when parents recognize this willingness to cooperate. Banking on this natural desire, parents can allow children to grow up without pushing or threatening them continually, since generally these attitudes work against what children will do for parents instinctively. What is needed is only a little more patience and respect for differences in children.

Neither overly harsh nor overly sympathetic, parents can let their children mature naturally while letting them gain a realistic view of life. Effective parents do not rob youngsters of the benefits derived from making their own mistakes. Standing by instead of interfering can be more difficult for parents who do not wish to see their children experience pain, but it is necessary if they are ever to become adults.

Parents also civilize children through helping them recognize both the potentials and boundaries to living. A parent does not help a child by letting him believe he can do anything he wants to do any more than by squelching opportunities for him to explore his potential. Not only discipline but limit-setting is supportive of a child's capabilities.

The best way for parents to teach children responsibility is for them to be responsible themselves. Offspring learn more through observing the behavior of parents than they do through admonitions or threats although, of course, they may be used at times. When youngsters discover that everyone has an equal place in the family, they are less apt to demand special treatment. Thus parents are not required to be full-time entertainers for their children, give them everything they want or do all the things they wish. They can learn to care for themselves as others in the family do.

Responsible behavior is learned when parents make their

youngsters feel important, but not more so than the parents themselves. Children cannot completely monopolize their parents' time and resources and still succeed in growing up. They need to understand that adults must have time for their special companionship apart from their offspring and that there are limits to what parents can do for them.

Parents need time for privacy, energy for their career and adult companionship. Times together with children can be thoroughly enjoyed and appreciated, but likewise times apart should be enjoyed without feeling guilt that their youngsters are being neglected. Learning that parents have a life apart from theirs gives children a realistic view of life.

*Intimacy is contagious and transmitted unknowingly between parents and youngsters.* Quiet talks, reading books together, playing games, mealtimes and bedtimes all convey to children the warm side of life. Many parents needlessly scold themselves for the mistakes they make with youngsters, or for not spending enough time with them, when they do not recognize that children will often dominate as much of their lives as they will allow.

Parents today have taken too much blame for youth's problems and need to give themselves credit for what they have done decently. Many difficulties with children right themselves once parents regain self-confidence. Showing affection, being available to listen or doing things together then comes easier. Intimidated or guilt-ridden parents make parenting hard work when it should be pleasurable. In fact, parents can even relearn some of the joys of intimate living through their offspring. Lost spontaneity can be regained. Phony façades can be removed. Then they can again love freely and openly without shame or embarrassment. Not only can children be allies when they encourage parents to do their job properly, but they can easily seduce parents into revealing their human side—a benefit for both parties.

The family is still the breeding ground for people who are responsible, care about their neighbors and know what it means to be closely connected to others. It is the place where people learn to be human in the finest sense of the word. For these reasons it will never die, any more than will mankind's hopes for a world that is at peace with itself.

## Checking Your Relationship

1. Have you and your partner been able to decide on the number of children you wish to have?
2. Are you agreed that both parents are necessary in child care?
3. Are you flexible enough to be either firm or tender with your children depending on the situation? Can your partner do the same?
4. If you are divorced, have you and your ex-spouse worked out a reasonable plan for the care of your children? Can you do so even though you are unable to be friendly in other ways?
5. What are your unique abilities as a parent? What are your partner's?
6. Everyone knows the difficulties involved in having children. But do you think there are advantages that make the effort worthwhile?
7. What kind of people would you like your children to grow up to be?
8. What are the most important things you would like to pass on to your children before they leave home?
9. When overburdened with difficulties with children, have you and your partner been able to work together to handle problems? Are you aware of the numerous agencies in your community that can help you in raising healthy and happy children?
10. Can you give yourself and your partner credit for the decent things you have done for your children?

# 14

## Tender Is
## the Knot

PLAIN OLD-FASHIONED MARRIAGE WITH ALL ITS SHORT-comings and limitations, even today, is still the simplest path to substantial and lasting intimacy. Living together, except as a prelude to marriage, is often fraught with legal, financial and emotional complications. Divorce is never simple, and its financial and emotional costs are often overwhelming. Remarriage can also be difficult for all the parties concerned, especially when children are involved.

Recent trend reports of demographers suggest that some of the social upheaval in family living is easing. The divorce rate has stabilized and the remarriage rate has decreased. Marriage is still preferred as a way of life, though it has been overhauled and streamlined, and is being entered at a later age by young people.

Demographers further state that marriages of the future will be different in two major respects—more couples will elect to remain childless and most pairs will live together before marriage. Otherwise, marriage and family ties will remain basically the same, as the chief source of intimacy for couples, and there are indications that extended family contacts will grow in importance.

Such reports are no guarantee that marriage as an institution will last forever. Unless the lessons of intimacy are learned, it cannot survive for long. Tradition or other external supports are not enough to keep people together. To maintain a marital relationship both partners must be competent as intimate companions. Adulthood and maturity are essential to a viable relationship. As Baroness Leonie Ungern-Stunberg said fifty years ago, "Marriage in the future can survive only if borne by a personal relationship from human being to human being." Change is always painful. The whirlwinds of our society today are blowing us out of traditional molds, but the new is still unfamiliar. In the midst of change the internal bonding processes remain the same—caring for one another, accepting differences in each person, learning to communicate, developing fairness, learning to be free together and finding intimacy. These are the processes that allow a relationship to work at its best. Intimacy is kept alive through the continuity of marriage, which offers a haven from aloneness and alienation.

Though vulnerable and exposed, marriage still offers the best hope for civilizing and humanizing all of us. It may be battered and beaten, but it is not dead. People still choose it as a primary source of satisfaction in living. Less bound by tradition and stereotypical form, it can now be chosen more freely and enjoyed more openly as a way of life.

# What Is Intimacy? A Check List

THE FOLLOWING IS BASED ON THE SIX KEY ELEMENTS necessary for a lasting intimate relationship. Check one of the three possible statements under each heading.

PART I  Learning to Love

1 True love
   A is something that lasts a lifetime.
   B is based on liking and knowing a partner.
   C means that saying "I love you" is enough.
2 A love relationship
   A is always complicated and usually leads to pain.
   B can be enjoyed simply at times.
   C doesn't have to be realistic very often.
3 Being "in love"
   A remains constant throughout the lifetime of marriage.
   B is enjoyable but mates usually move on to a different kind of love.
   C never happens to intelligent people.

PART II  Learning to Accept Differences in a Companion

1 In a good relationship partners
   A always find companionship by doing things together.
   B respect and sometimes enjoy each other's differences.
   C always try to prevent conflict by pleasing their mates.
2 Companions who find intimacy together
   A overlook the differences they see in each other.

B are able to recognize "irreconcilable differences" between them.

C find romantic love more important than friendship.

3 Love makes it possible to

A change the characteristics you don't like in your partner after marriage.

B take your companion at face value.

C depend on your mate to always understand you.

## PART III  Learning to Communicate

1 Companions have good communication if

A they know what the other is going to say before he or she says it.

B they openly share their feelings and thoughts about most things.

C they tell each other everything they think and feel.

2 The feelings aroused while communicating with a mate

A have little to do with solving problems.

B are always an important part of decision-making.

C have to be given special consideration in dealing with a female partner because women are more emotional.

3 Quarreling with a mate over trivial matters

A indicates poor communication.

B can clear the air so rational discussions are possible.

C usually indicates what really bothers him or her.

## PART IV  Learning to be Fair as a Couple

1 When beginning a love relationship, most couples

A understand one another's assumptions about living together.

B gradually find out what a partner expects.

C are better off telling a partner how everything is going to be from the beginning.

2 Negotiation is a part of living together

A only when one does not wish to make a commitment.

B throughout the lifetime of a union.

C only when problems arise.

3 Learning to be fair in a relationship means

A deciding who gets his or her way more often.

B one wants as much satisfaction in living for a partner as one does for himself or herself.

C giving much more than one receives.

## PART V   Learning to Be Free Together

1 Personal freedom means
   A one has to be single.
   B freedom with a mate where individuality in each is respected.
   C doing all the things one wishes without considering the consequences.
2 Living together is different from marriage because
   A one does not have to make any kind of commitment.
   B sometimes one's legal rights are not protected.
   C it doesn't result in grief when you break up.
3 Emotional freedom is found more often when you are able to
   A date as many people as you wish.
   B be self-directed though married.
   C get away from responsibilities with other people.

## PART VI   Finding Intimacy Together

1 Intimacy indicates
   A you have a good sex relationship.
   B you can be close to your mate easily most of the time.
   C your relationship with your partner is always the same.
2 Closeness with a partner comes when you
   A have done everything to please your mate.
   B are able to simply enjoy one another's company.
   C ask your partner to be more affectionate.
3 Intimacy has nothing to do with
   A feeling equal to your partner.
   B differences between mates in abilities and intelligence.
   C self-acceptance.

*How to Score:* The correct answer for all eighteen questions is *B*. Check the six headings to see on which set of three you did the best. These are indicators of your strongest areas in an intimate relationship. The area where you missed one, two or three under a heading is what you and your mate need to discuss further.

# A Quiz on Aspects of Intimacy

MARK EACH OF THE FOLLOWING STATEMENTS AS TRUE OR FALSE.

1. Sex causes most intimate problems.
2. Companionship means doing things together.
3. Compromise is the cardinal principle of living together.
4. You can make your partner happy if you try hard enough.
5. Love in a relationship means a partner will always be fair.
6. Jealousy is always bad in a relationship.
7. Change rarely occurs in a good relationship.
8. You should never say anything to hurt your partner's feelings.
9. There is no grief when a living-together arrangement breaks up.
10. Humor doesn't help a couple when serious problems arise.
11. Equality in marriage means partners split all duties fifty-fifty.
12. Absorbing careers and hobbies usually detract from an intimate relationship.
13. A love relationship is never simple.
14. Stubbornness in a partner is a bad quality in living together.
15. A good marriage never becomes boring.
16. Good sex always indicates true intimacy.
17. Partners with irreconcilable differences can't live together.
18. An affair has little effect on a good marriage.

19. Couples with more money have better relationships than couples with less.
20. Usually when a marriage fails, one partner is in the right and the other is the wrong.
21. Couples should always work out their serious problems immediately.
22. If you live with a partner long enough, you know how they think and feel even before they speak.
23. Most troubles in intimate relationships stem from the fact that men and women are different in their needs, emotions and intellect.
24. The harder you try, the more you get out of any living-together arrangement.
25. Well-behaved children are a sign that parents love one another as well as their children.

*How to Score:* All of the statements on this quiz are false. They reflect many of the misconceptions held by couples which lead to difficulties in intimate living. If you have twenty or more correct answers, chances are you make a good intimate companion. Fifteen or more correct answers are good, but perhaps you should rethink some attitudes. Fewer than fifteen correct answers indicates you need to work on your attitudes, the ones that interfere with your enjoying intimate living.

# About the Author

HERBERT ZEROF is director of the Marriage and Family Institute in Charlotte, North Carolina, and was formerly a consultant to the U.S. Navy and the National Institutes of Mental Health in Washington, D.C. A past president of the North Carolina Association of Marriage and Family Counselors, he is a member of the American Psychological Association and the American Association of Marriage and Family Counselors. He received his doctorate at the University of Pennsylvania, and has taught at its School of Medicine as well as at other institutions, including Swarthmore College and the University of North Carolina.

Dr. Zerof is married to Aletta McDonald, and they have two children, Linda and Cheryl.